COME TO LIFE!

Your Guide to Self-Discovery

Helping Youth With Autism and Learning Differences Shape Their Futures

THOMAS W. ILAND & EMILY D. ILAND

Copyright © 2017 by
Thomas W. Iland and Emily D. Iland

All rights reserved. This book or any portion thereof may not be reproduced or used in any manner whatsoever without the express written permission of the publisher, except for the use of brief quotations in a book review.

ISBN: 978-0-9768222-7-1

Printed in the USA
First Printing: July, 2017
Second Printing: September, 2017

Layout: Rowe Publishing.
Cover Design: Plaid Lizard Designs
Cover image: Daniil Pskov

Published and Distributed by Porterville Press
26893 Bouquet Canyon Rd. C-333
Saugus, CA 91350
661-347-8557

To order copies of this book or to learn about presentations by Tom and Emily, visit www.ThomasIland.com and www.EmilyIland.com

Disclaimer

The content provided in this book represents general information and the opinions of the authors for educational and informational purposes only. We are not psychological or medical professionals, and the content is not intended as medical, legal, educational or personal advice.

Readers are urged to use independent judgment regarding the information or resources discussed herein and/or seek the advice of medical, legal or educational professionals to determine a course of action that is appropriate for a particular individual or circumstance. There is no warranty or endorsement of any resource, service or method mentioned herein, nor the content of third-party websites.

Dedication

This book is dedicated to you, the reader, whether you're a young person finding your way in the world, or you're an ally in that person's journey. Whatever your personal circumstances, we hope that this book will provide you with guidance and inspiration.

Kathy,
I hope this book helps you become your best self.
May you know yourself, love yourself and be yourself!
Jon

Acknowledgments

We're grateful to all the teachers, therapists and other professionals who have worked with Tom and had such a positive impact on his life. We want to thank everyone who taught him the many wise things he has learned. In particular we want to thank the late Marty Lieberman, who made such a difference in Tom's life.

Thank you to Steve and Danny Iland and Lisa Iland Hilbert for your love and patience. Thank you to Barbara Doyle, Ivor Weiner and other family members, friends, colleagues and mentors who have offered support and encouragement to us both throughout the years.

Thank you to everyone who assisted with the production of this book, including everyone who read our drafts and offered suggestions. We appreciate our graphic designers Sherri Rowe and Dianne Porter, who created *Come to Life*'s visual appeal. Thanks to Kyle Duffy for assistance with outreach and marketing.

Contents

Preface by Tom ix

Introduction by Emily 1

Chapter One: Drive Your Life Forward 5

Chapter Two: Know Yourself 21

Chapter Three: Love Yourself 55

Chapter Four: Be Yourself 69

Chapter Five: Find Yourself 87

Chapter Six: Find Your Voice 115

Conclusion 145

References 151

Bibliography 153

About the Authors 157

Preface by Tom

Are you ready to *Come to Life!*? The journey from leaving school to becoming an adult can be a challenge for anyone. It can be even more difficult for teens and young adults like me with a learning difference or a disability. I hope that reading this book takes you a step closer to making a better life for yourself or someone you care about.

As a person on the autism spectrum, I've had my share of difficulties, whether it was going to college, living on my own, finding a job or keeping a job. It took a very long time to learn how to make friends, find a girlfriend, and figure out where I belong. With the support of my family and others, I found that I was capable of accomplishing just about anything that I set my mind and heart to.

I have discovered some helpful information and ideas that I want to share with others in a similar situation. In my very first days of community college, I had a life-changing realization—Life no longer came to me … **it was up to ME to come to life!** I realized that I had to be active, not passive, to get what I wanted in life. I had relied on my parents and teachers for many years, for many things, and now I wanted to be more independent.

I worked with my parents and teachers to put together a road map to my future. My team worked with me on the social skills, communication skills, organization skills and life skills that I needed to be successful. I also got help with academics and, when I was 24, I earned a Bachelor's degree in accounting from California State University, Northridge!

In the two years that followed, I worked hard to become a certified public accountant (CPA), a respected title in the world of finance. I spent months preparing for the Uniform CPA Examination, one of the hardest tests there is. Fortunately, I passed all four sections, some after many attempts.

I hoped that I would love my career in accounting, but after seven years of working for different companies, I did not feel that accounting was right for me. My heart was elsewhere. I believe my real place in life is helping others find their way in the world, as I have. So I decided to walk away from my accounting job, a good salary and benefits to pursue my passion of helping people like you.

I know that there are many people, especially others on the autism spectrum, who don't know what to do with their lives. There are also people, disability or not, who know what they want but are not sure how to get it. Some simply give up because they don't believe they have the knowledge or skills to do what it takes to succeed. They are stuck in "neutral" rather than moving forward on the road of life towards their goals.

I have been through many of the struggles you are likely going through right now and I have overcome many of them! To help you with this process, I will share my journey of self-discovery and explain my mantra: **Know Yourself. Love Yourself. Be Yourself.** I'll tell you about different experiences I had, and what I learned from them. I hope that these stories will be helpful to you.

I am here to convey the message that you, too, **can** take control of your own unique situation and begin to live the life of your dreams. Are you ready to shift your life from "neutral" to "drive?" Buckle up and enjoy the ride with me!

Introduction by Emily

Come to Life! is written by a young adult or *self-advocate* for peers who need more understanding and support to find their way in the world. I added my perspective as a mom and an educator to also make this a practical guide for "allies," the parents, caregivers, educators, service providers and other professionals who are helping youth in the transition to adulthood, readers like you!

The goal of *Come to Life!* is to help youth discover important truths about themselves, truths that are at the heart of becoming an adult. When youth are more self-aware they can be more involved in shaping their own futures. Helping youth with the process of self-discovery is one of the most impactful things allies can do.

Adulthood can be defined as the point in time when young people start a life of their own. They take on new roles and responsibilities such as moving out of the family home, finding work, getting married and starting a family. In the past, these adult milestones were often expected to happen at a particular age, like 18 or 21. Now, because of changes in the economy and society, starting out in life is taking longer than it did in the past. The process may also be different than it was a generation or two ago when many young people were "kicked out of the house" when they turned 18.

The process of becoming an adult, or *transition to adulthood*, can be particularly challenging for millennials, youth born between the early 1980s and the early 2000s (also called "Generation Next"). My son Tom is a millennial who grew up with additional challenges related to his autism. Looking at him today as a successful adult, it is hard to imagine the struggles he experienced as he grew up. In fact, those struggles affected his life and our family life every single day. We all had to do a lot of work to grow and move forward.

Many people ask us questions like, "What are some of the things you did to help Tom be successful?" or, "What are your secrets to success?" This is what gave us the idea to write a book together, to share some of the things we have learned along the way to help other young people who are growing up.

When I asked Tom what his "secrets to success" were, he answered, "Know Yourself. Love Yourself. Be Yourself." I was stunned by this incredible reply. I asked him to tell me more.

As I typed while Tom talked, we captured his ideas and the book began to write itself. I asked questions to explore and expand on each topic. We discussed specific turning points in his life that had a lasting impact on him. Most of the time you hear Tom's voice, and in some cases you will hear our blended voice, coming straight from our conversations.

We had a great collaborative energy in the writing process. I contributed activities to support his vision, and added content to the chapter on advocacy because I am a professional advocate. We worked together to search out additional resources for youth and allies to explore. But to be clear, Tom is in the driver's seat in the creation of this book and I am navigating from the passenger seat!

This is **not** a personal account of Tom's life. Rather it is a series of revelations and discoveries he made from his experiences (both the good and the not-so-good ones). Tom shares the insight he gained in the process to help and inspire others, and highlights specific examples to guide others on their path to the future.

In the first few chapters, Tom explains his mantra so young readers can make it their own. The activities will help readers discover and organize important information about themselves.

As we looked back on his past for the "secrets to success," we realized that Tom was very fortunate to have many opportunities outside of the classroom that helped him learn and grow. We came up with the idea of e^3 which stands for "Explore. Experience. Evolve." We'll explain more about this in the hope that the e^3 model can help youth find direction for their lives and realize their true potential.

All of this leads to the final chapter, "Find Your Voice," where we discuss how to help youth transform into self-advocates. Young people need to be prepared to recognize and express what they want and need for themselves. Youth who are taught to advocate for themselves often have better outcomes in their adult lives, especially in the area of work, than those who don't (NSTTAC, 2015).

Come to Life! can benefit any young person, but if someone is older and never had the chance to actively discover themselves, *Come to Life!* can help them, too! We intentionally designed *Come to Life!* as a *prequel* to coordinated, comprehensive transition services for students in special education, who have an Individual Education Plan (IEP) or a 504 Plan. You can imagine it is ideal for young adults in transition and adaptive skills programs, too.

Youth who have engaged in an active process of self-discovery can become true partners in their IEP meetings, transition planning or future planning. They can come to the meeting table with a clearer understanding of themselves and well-considered answers to the questions that drive the planning process (instead of a lot of "I don't knows!").

We are excited that *Come to Life!* can help anyone with exceptional needs, and want to point out that we designed the book with the particular needs of youth with Autism Spectrum Disorder (ASD) in mind. We are very familiar with the significant obstacles facing youth on the spectrum during transition. They are experiencing greater difficulties getting started in life compared to peers who don't have a disability. Adults with ASD are also experiencing poorer outcomes compared to adults with other disabilities (Roux et al., 2015). The information and activities in *Come to Life!* have been carefully designed to be appropriate for individuals with ASD, and relevant to them.

We also know that there is a great deal of diversity among young people in special education, particularly individuals on the autism spectrum. We hope you will adapt the information and activities in *Come to Life!* as needed to assist youth of all abilities in the process of self-discovery so that their plans for the future are true to themselves. It is clearly worth the effort to help them find ways to discover and express their strengths, needs and desires, share their opinions and make their own choices!

Feel free to be creative when you use the material, whether you model first for the young person, ask them to talk instead of write, or use other accommodations to make it work! You may assist youth who are more significantly impacted by their disability by using strategies like narrowing the field of options, giving personal examples, simplifying language, using communication devices or modifying in other appropriate ways.

Tom and I hope that *Come to Life!* will serve as a step-by-step guide for self-advocates and allies, helping youth transition more successfully to life. We hope you will find inspiration and useful information in these pages and enjoy the process of self-discovery together!

P.S. We know that allies are likely to want more information about how to improve transition planning. We will address that topic in Volume II in the *Come to Life!* series. Please visit our websites for more information and updates, www.ThomasIland.com and www.EmilyIland.com.

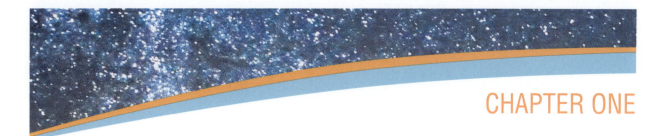

CHAPTER ONE

Drive Your Life Forward

Life After High School

When I first attended classes at my local community college, I quickly realized that things were going to be very different from high school. In high school, life comes to you. You pretty much just have to show up and do what is asked of you.

- A computer prints out your schedule.

- Teachers give you the books you need; you return them at the end of the semester.

- Time is managed for you; you change class when the bell rings.

- Your routine is usually the same five days a week.

- You get used to knowing when and where you will see your friends.

- You can talk to teachers before or after class, or stay after school to ask questions.

- Your parents and counselor make sure you are doing what you need to do.

Things are very different after high school when you are suddenly considered an adult. In college, I had to figure out what classes to take, on what schedule and with which professors.

- I had to figure out which books I needed, find them in the bookstore and pay for them.

- I had to manage my time going to class, doing assignments and preparing for tests (no one was checking on me!).
- I had to make an appointment to talk with professors.
- I had to plan when to see friends since everyone had their own schedule.

Come to Life!

Before I got there, I wasn't really aware of how different community college life is compared to high school. Once I experienced it for myself, I had a major revelation: I found out I couldn't just wait for life to come to me ... **I had to come to life!**

Whether in community college or any other aspect of adult life, I realized that I needed to be responsible for myself. I saw the importance of taking charge of my future and making my own choices, rather than letting other people manage my life.

I didn't know it at the time, but I was beginning to explore the idea of *self-determination*: I have the right to take my life in a direction that is right for me. I have to be the driver in the driver's seat of the car, taking my life in the direction I want to go. Not in the passenger seat, not in the back seat ... **I can be in control.**

Believe in Yourself

Many people on the autism spectrum love super-heroes. I'm a huge fan of Batman. For one thing, he always has a goal and a plan. He also has a utility belt with all the right tools for the job. And he has Alfred, his trusty go-to person who lets him talk things through, gives him good advice and keeps his spirits up.

Humans have amazing powers to achieve things, too, especially when you believe that you can accomplish them. I'm here to tell you that:

- You have the power to become your best self.
- You have the power to find your own happiness.
- You have the power to make choices and shape your own life.

You just have to be brave enough to take steps in the right direction, even if it is not easy. It can be motivating to know that your hard work can help you get something that you want for yourself.

Self-efficacy is a **belief** in your own power to control different aspects of your life and have an effect on how things turn out.

- Self-efficacy is recognizing your ability to do what you need to do to reach your goals.
- Believing in yourself and realizing that YOU have the power to accomplish what you want will increase the likelihood of getting what you want or need.

Who Are Your Allies?

At first, I thought that being in control of my life meant I had to do everything by myself. However, belief in yourself and your abilities does not mean you have to go it alone. It is important to ask for help; it is not a sign of weakness. It makes more sense to learn to drive from someone who already knows how, right? The same goes for other areas of life where you can learn from others *and* with others.

At some point in my teenage years, I realized that it was a good idea to find people who could help me learn new skills and make decisions. Parents, brothers and sisters, teachers, therapists and others in your life who want to help you are your *allies*. These important people are like your personal team, caring people who can share advice and guidance. They can help you and you can help them, too; that's called *interdependence*.

For example, I wanted to have a girlfriend. I found out I had to learn how to be a good friend to a girl before I had a girlfriend because most romantic relationships are based on friendship. My sister, Lisa, was a good source for advice about the dating scene.

She told me that girls often want to date a guy who is attractive not only on the outside, but also the inside. This means having a nice personality (inside) and being well-groomed (outside). This knowledge motivated me to be "date-worthy." I appreciate the help Lisa gave me to understand this and I returned the favor by helping her with her math.

Once I had a better idea of what girls looked for in a guy, I was inspired to take on positive traits and learn new skills. For me, this meant learning to be clean and healthy, becoming a good speaker and listener, learning to cook and dance, treating my family right, etc.

All of this took time (years!). When it was not easy, I reminded myself I was working towards my own goal and my own happiness. Taking control of things I could affect helped me feel smarter and more powerful, which had a positive effect in the dating scene. Yes, I am happy to say I met my goal. I have had several girlfriends (one at a time!).

Belief that I am responsible for my own destiny, that I am capable and that I can do what I want empowered me to go after what I wanted and ask for what I needed. I accepted help from my allies to learn to do new things and achieve many accomplishments. As a result, I gained confidence and was able to do even "braver" things such as speak in front of an audience or join a club.

You might need help to reach your goals, too. A student I know was having difficulty going to his professor to ask for help. He told me he liked *Marvel* comic books. I knew the X-MEN were in *Marvel* comic books and I suggested that he pretend that he was an X-Man going to see Professor Xavier for help. His face lit up! This analogy gave him the confidence he needed to do something that was hard for him and find his own power as well. I was glad to be there for him.

Who can help you get what you want for yourself? Please accept and embrace the support of parents, family members and friends who can help you get ready for life! They may have ideas and information to help you. Build relationships with teachers, classmates, tutors and mentors who can help you build skills and learn what you need to know. Find professionals who can provide the services and supports you need.

Consider these people your allies, people who support your dreams and can help you achieve them. Many times, when people work together with a common goal in mind, they can come up with some great ideas that they might not come up with on their own. Team players and teamwork can be a real benefit to you, whether you need help figuring out what you want in life, or planning the steps you need to take to reach your dreams.

Now It's Your Turn

It takes time to prepare yourself to be in control of your life. To help you get started, you might like to explore any or all of these activities. Your allies can also do these things with you to help you get ready to drive *your* life forward.

Activity 1A

Who's My Superhero?

Superheroes are not real people but they can be really inspiring. You may identify with Batman like I do. You might like another superhero such as Superman, The Flash, Wolverine, Spider-Man, Iron Man, Captain America, Thor, Hulk, Wonder Woman, Black Widow, Storm, Batgirl or Supergirl. Choose one of these or your own favorite for this activity.

How is your superhero a good role model for you? You can use this *infographic* (visual tool) to write down the good things that your favorite superhero has going for him or her.

- First, I share my example to show how to do the activity.
- Then, there's a blank infographic for you to complete.

When you get to the end of this book, you will notice that this first activity and the last activity are connected. It will all make sense when you read the information that comes in between!

Activity 1A — Tom's Example

Who's My Superhero?

Superhero: name	Batman
Superpower: special skills	Smart, good at planning and strategy, expert on criminal behavior, great at martial arts
Purpose: what she/he does	Uses strength and ingenuity to generate fear in criminals and fight injustice
Special tools	Batsuits for various scenarios and environments, Batmobile, Batwing (plane), Batboat, Bat Signal, utility belt, grapple guns, Batarangs, customized antidotes and weapons
Assets: other things the superhero has going for him or her	Batcave underneath Wayne Manor. Alter ego (Bruce Wayne) and Wayne family are well-respected in Gotham City. Lots of money to spend on his mission. Access to resources at Wayne Enterprises.

Activity 1A — Tom's Example (continued)

Weakness(es): things that take away the hero's power or distract from his or her mission 	Bruce Wayne is human and can be killed just like any other man. People that Bruce Wayne loves can be taken hostage by criminals. Feelings of guilt and trauma associated with his parents' murder.
Allies: people who help 	Alfred Pennyworth (Wayne family butler), Police Commissioner James Gordon, Wayne Enterprises CEO Lucius Fox, Dick Grayson (Robin)
Role model: How is my superhero a good role model for me? 	• Batman strives to be stronger and at least one step ahead of his enemies (very proactive). • He fights for the greater good while having his limits (no guns, no killing). • He is not afraid to take on difficult tasks. • He has a very high level of discipline and does not quit until his mission is completed. • He has gathered the tools he needs and relies on his allies to help him.

Activity 1A (continued)

Who's My Superhero?

Superhero: name	
Superpower: special skills	
Purpose: what she/he does	
Special tools	
Assets: other things the superhero has going for him or her	

14 • Come to Life! Your Guide to Self-Discovery

Activity 1A (continued)

Weakness(es): things that take away the hero's power or distract from his or her mission	
Allies: people who help	
Role model: How is my superhero a good role model for me?	

Activity 1B

What Seat Are You In?

Self-determination means that you have the **right** to take your life in the direction that you want. A good analogy is being in the driver's seat of a car, going in the direction you want to go. Take a look at this infographic that describes different seats in the car of life. What seat are you in? Is that the seat you want to be in?

This activity can help you figure out whether you are driving your life forward, or if someone else is. Maybe in some situations you are in the driver's seat, and in other situations, you're not. Don't worry, it takes time and practice to be the driving force in your own life. Just like learning to drive a car, you need to build skills and knowledge to take your life in the direction you want to go.

This activity is a starting point to figure out where things are at now, and if you want to make a change in the months and years to come. Talk with your allies about what you can do to take more responsibility and control of your life. You can also discuss skills you need to build or information you need to know to get behind the steering wheel of your life!

Activity 1B (continued)

What Seat Am I In?

In the journey of life, which seat am I in?	Driver's Seat? Passenger Seat? Back Seat?
Is that the seat I want to be in?	YES NO
How can I make a change to drive my life forward?	

Driver's seat: I know where I am going. I make important choices and decisions. I am in control of the journey.

Passenger seat: I am along for the ride, but someone else is in control of the journey. I may take the role of navigator, giving directions and telling the driver where to go.

Back seat: I let others take me along on their journey, but have little to do or say about it. I do not have control about where we are going or how to get there.

Chapter One • 17

Activity 1C

Who's On My Team?

You don't have to do everything on your own, now or in the future. It is OK to be *interdependent* and count on people who can help you learn and be successful. Family members like parents, grandparents, brothers, sisters, cousins or other relatives can be supportive. Teachers, therapists and other professionals can guide you. People your own age like friends, classmates or mentors could possibly help out. Other people in your life who want to help you are also your allies.

Who's On My Team?

I can fill out this infographic to identify my allies (people who can help me). I can use it to find someone to talk to when I need help, guidance or information.

ROLES	NAMES
Family members	
Teachers, therapists, and other professionals	
Friends, classmates, roommates	
Tutors, mentors, and other people in my life	

Come to Life! Your Guide to Self-Discovery

Resources

Websites — There are a lot of interesting resources online that can help you explore the ideas from this chapter. Here are a few suggestions.

- Best-selling author, speaker and coach Sue Brooke explains the importance of "Discovering Your 'I'" whether it be identity, inspiration, impact, intelligence…just to name a few!
  http://suebrooke.com/i-system-for-success/

- Rose Alexander offers eight helpful tips to help you discover yourself and what your purpose in life really is.
  http://www.lifescript.com/well-being/articles/b/begin_your_journey_of_self_discovery.aspx

- Wayne Lee, known for providing "Entertainment with a Message," explains 10 steps towards improving your confidence and empowering yourself in the process.
  http://www.waynelee.com/members/10-tips-for-self-discovery-and-confidence/

Videos — Here are a few suggestions of online videos that can help you explore some of the ideas in this chapter.

- *Discover Yourself* is a motivational video that can give viewers insight into the lives they are living, and discover how to be happy and productive.
  https://www.youtube.com/watch?v=rrcTR5ovBYk

- This TED talk with philosopher Julian Baggini discusses questions about personal identity, including, "Is there a real you?"
  https://www.ted.com/talks/julian_baggini_is_there_a_real_you?language=en

- Actress Thandie Newton of *The Pursuit of Happyness*, *Beloved*, and *Crash* discusses embracing her "otherness." She talks about her unique background, growing up with many different cultures, and explains how this led to playing many different roles in her movie career.
  https://www.ted.com/talks/thandie_newton_embracing_otherness_embracing_ myself?language=en

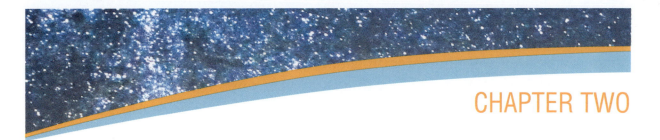

CHAPTER TWO

Know Yourself

Discover Yourself

Self-discovery is a natural part of becoming an adult: learning to understand yourself and discover your place in the world. In the process of self-discovery, you ask and answer key questions: Who am I? What do I want? What makes me happy? Who will be part of my life? What do I want to do with my life?

Taking the time to explore the answers to these questions can give direction to your life. It is a chance to decide what is right for you. In other words, the process of self-discovery helps you map your own path to happiness. You can get a clearer picture of what you want to do for work and for fun.

You can get a sense of belonging, find where you fit in and be appreciated—whether it is about work, college, living arrangements or social situations. You can widen your social network and have meaningful relationships with others. With a vision and a plan, you are more likely to have a positive outcome instead of leaving decisions about your future to chance or to someone else.

Words to Live By

I came up with a mantra that captures the meaning of self-discovery:

> **Know Yourself. Love Yourself. Be Yourself.**

Know Yourself means understanding your own strengths and challenges. *Love Yourself* means recognizing your value as a human being, and accepting yourself as a unique person who has strengths and challenges like everyone else. Finally, *Be Yourself* means being brave enough to adapt and grow to become the best version of yourself.

Learning to know yourself, love yourself and be yourself can give you knowledge and confidence to make your way in the world. Over time, I have become successful doing these things and it has made a huge difference in my life. Here's an infographic to help you remember these ideas.

Know Yourself	Love Yourself	Be Yourself
Understand your own strengths and challenges.	Recognize your value as a human being. Accept yourself as a unique person who has strengths and challenges like everyone else.	Be willing to adapt and grow to become the best version of yourself.

This chapter will explore *Know Yourself*, the first aspect of self-discovery or personal development. I will offer some practical ideas about how to make progress in this area. The chapters that follow will explore *Love Yourself* and *Be Yourself*.

I encourage you to take the time to embrace the process of self-discovery to help you know who you are, what you want and what you need. Your allies can help with the process so that you are better prepared to reach your own goals and dreams. Check out the infographic *Discovering ME!* that sums up what we will be talking about in the rest of the chapter.

Discovering ME!

IDEA	WHAT IT MEANS	BENEFIT TO ME
Self-discovery	Learning to understand myself, discover my place in the world and make connections with others.	Prepares me to take action and work towards getting the life I want for myself.
Self-awareness	Understanding my personality, feelings and desires. Figuring out what I like, what inspires me and what I want out of life.	Helps me become the best version of myself that I can be. Helps me speak up to get what I want and need.
Recognize abilities and areas for improvement	Identifying my strengths and things I'm good at. Being aware of areas where I have room to grow or skills I need to work on.	I can use my strengths as tools for success. Identifying areas for growth can help me work on those things.

Chapter Two • 23

Know Yourself

Who are you? There can be many answers to this question and the answers can change over time. The answer can be as simple as "I am a man." The answer can focus on what you do such as "I am a student" or "I am an accountant." The answer can also be more detailed and include aspects of your personality or character such as, "I am a kind person," "I am a hard worker" or "I am determined to reach my goals."

Who Are You?

A friend taught me a really useful exercise that helped me understand who I am. You might like to find a partner and test it out. You can use a voice recorder app on your phone, a regular tape recorder or even a video camera to capture the conversation. You can also use the infographic we made and ask your partner to write down your answers.

The process of self-discovery includes figuring out what inspires you and what you want out of life. I hope you find, like I did, that answering the same questions over and over helps you dig deeper to discover and describe who you really are.

Here are the instructions:

1. Set a timer for 90 seconds.
2. Have a partner ask you the question, "Who are you?"
3. Answer the question.
4. Have your partner ask you the same question, again and again. Give a different answer each time until time is up.
5. Switch roles, and ask your partner, "Who are you?" as many times as you can during their turn (90 seconds).

Then do the same thing with the other questions:

- What Motivates You?
- What Kind of Person Are You?
- What Do You Want In Life?

Activity 2A

Who Are You?

I can do this activity with a partner to help me know myself.
We can use this infographic to write down our answers, use a voice recorder, or both.

Who Am I?

What Motivates Me?

What Kind of Person Am I?

What Do I Want in Life?

Chapter Two • 25

Likes and Dislikes

Knowing yourself is closely related to an idea called *self-awareness*. Self-awareness means noticing things about yourself. Some of the easiest things to be aware of are things you like. Identifying what you like or need can help you get those things!

For example, when you go to the movies, you probably look for an open seat in a particular part of the movie theater. Maybe you like to sit in the last row with no one behind you. Maybe you like to be close to the speakers for better sound. These are examples of your *preferences*, which are things that you like and things that feel comfortable to you.

It is equally important to identify the things that you do not like or want, and things that don't work for you. Things that you don't like or that make you uncomfortable can be called *aversions*. Back to the movie theater example, maybe you dislike sitting in the front row because you have to lean your head back to see the screen. Maybe you dislike sitting near someone who is texting during the movie.

It's a good idea to start noticing what feels uncomfortable or annoying to you. Recognizing your aversions helps you avoid them, if possible, or work around them when you can. What if you don't like sitting in the front row, and only front row seats are left when you come into the theater? To avoid that, you may want to be one of the first in line for the next show when plenty of seats are available, rather than taking a seat you do not prefer.

Preferences and Aversions

The example of the movie theater can help you become aware of your comfort level in other areas of your life, whether it is food choices, work environments or clothes. In any situation, you can identify your preferences (things you like and want for yourself) and your aversions (things you do not like and would rather avoid if you can).

For example, I have had a variety of living arrangements. I have lived at home with my parents and I've lived in an apartment alone. I've lived with a roommate and I've lived with a girlfriend.

Having experienced these different situations, I've discovered that I prefer to live on my own. Living alone allows for privacy. I can come and go as I please. I have plenty of room and I can put my things where I want them.

I learned that having a roommate who is messy, does not do his share of the chores or does not pay his rent on time does not work for me. Knowing this about myself empowers me to live the way I prefer. It also helps me avoid situations that are awkward or uncomfortable.

Here's an infographic that shows how I identified my likes and dislikes to help make a decision about my living arrangements:

What I Like and What I Don't Like

Self-awareness means you notice certain things about yourself. Preferences are things you like or need. Identifying your preferences helps you get what you like or need.

You also need to identify the things that you don't like or want, and things that don't work for you (aversions). Recognizing things you don't want helps you avoid them, if possible, or work around them.

I used the infographic that follows to summarize some preferences for my living situation (things I like and want for myself) and aversions (things I don't like and would rather avoid if I can). Take a look at this model. You can also identify your preferences and aversions for any situation in life, whether it is food choices, work environments or wardrobe options.

What I Like and What I Don't Like

LIKES (Preferences) 👍	DISLIKES (Aversions) 👎
What I want: To be comfortable and happy in my home	**What I don't want:** To be uncomfortable or unhappy with my living arrangement
What I like: Having privacy	**What I don't like:** People coming and going at all hours and waking me up when I'm sleeping
What is good for me: Feeling happy in my own space	**What is not good for me:** Getting frustrated with roommates who don't do their share of chores
What works for me: To live on my own	**What doesn't work for me:** Sharing my space, especially with people who don't pay their rent on time or aren't responsible roommates

Get the idea? You can list your likes and dislikes for any aspect of your life! Thinking through what works for you and what does not work for you can help you be more comfortable and even reduce stress. Here's an infographic you can use to summarize some of your preferences and aversions. You can copy the page and fill it out about any area or topic.

What I Like and What I Don't Like	
LIKES (Preferences) 👍	**DISLIKES (Aversions)** 👎
What I want:	What I don't want:
What I like:	What I don't like:
What is good for me:	What is not good for me:
What works for me:	What doesn't work for me:

Strengths and Challenges

Another aspect of self-awareness is recognizing your abilities and areas for improvement. Everyone has strengths and challenges; it is nothing to be ashamed of. Some people call challenges "opportunities for improvement." This means that you have the chance to grow, learn or improve skills that are not so strong.

Becoming aware of what you are good at and *not* so good at can make a world of a difference in so many areas of daily life. For example, before I started a new job as an accountant at an avocado company in California, I thought about my own strengths and challenges. I knew that some of my strengths would serve me well. Being organized, on time, reliable and up-to-date on professional education would help me do my job. I also have a strong memory. I can remember a lot of information and many details.

On the other hand, I was also aware that certain things were hard for me in past jobs. This included fitting into a new work environment and figuring out what social rules I needed to follow. It was also a challenge to learn to communicate with my coworkers, especially when I needed help with work-related issues.

I went into my new job thinking about what I had learned from past work experiences and the kind of support I would need to succeed. With the help of a job coach, I was able to communicate this to my employer. Being aware of my strengths and challenges helped me get some support in the areas where I needed improvement and do the job to the best of my ability.

Part of the pattern of strengths and challenges that I identified was related to me having autism. Recognizing both the positive and not-so-positive aspects of ASD and knowing how autism affects me were huge steps in the process of self-discovery. If you have ASD, attention deficit hyperactivity disorder (ADHD) or any other learning difference or disability, understanding what it means and knowing how it affects you will help you truly know yourself. I'll talk more about understanding your disability in the *Love Yourself* and *Be Yourself* sections of the book.

The infographic *Identifying My Strengths and Challenges* summarizes the strengths and challenges about my work-life balance. I hope it is a good example to help you recognize your own abilities and needs.

Identifying My Strengths and Challenges

Everyone has strengths and challenges; it is nothing to be ashamed of. Knowing what I'm good at or not so good at empowers me to work towards the life I want.

Identifying My Strengths and Challenges

Work Life

STRENGTHS (Tools I Can Use) ⊕	CHALLENGES (Opportunities for Improvement) ⊖
Organized	Adapting to a new work environment
On time and reliable	Figuring out how formal or informal a workplace is
Strong memory	Communicating with my coworkers on work-related issues
Up-to-date on professional education	Communicating with my coworkers on social topics
Follows rules	Decision-making and judgment

Chapter Two • 31

You might like to fill out this infographic to discover more about yourself. You can use it to look at strengths and challenges in different aspects of your life (family member, college student, worker, friend, etc.).

Identifying My Strengths and Challenges	
Everyone has strengths and challenges; it is nothing to be ashamed of. Knowing what I'm good at or not so good at empowers me to work towards the life I want.	
STRENGTHS (Tools I Can Use)	**CHALLENGES** (Opportunities for Improvement)

Mind and Body

Another aspect of knowing yourself, or *self-awareness*, is learning to recognize your physical or emotional state. One example is recognizing the physical signs that mean you have the flu. Another example is recognizing the signals in your mind or body that tell you that you're getting upset.

Our physical and emotional states can change quickly. Becoming aware of your physical and emotional states helps you *self-regulate*, or bring yourself back into balance. Everyone needs to learn ways to cope with everyday stresses, whether they are physical or emotional. I meditate every morning to start out the day feeling calm. I also learned to do slow breathing and quiet counting to give myself a moment to calm down when things are not going my way. It is helpful to have these kinds of tools in my toolbox ready for whenever I need them.

You may want to learn more about the things that can put your day (or your life) out of balance, and things that help you get back on track. The infographic *Being Aware of My Physical and Emotional Status* can help you become aware of some physical and emotional things that may affect you at any given moment. This can help you become more in-tune to your mind and body.

We also suggest some coping strategies in the infographic. You can learn about these or other options to help you manage your emotions or physical feelings (self-regulate). It's a good idea to practice using coping strategies *before* you're faced with a challenging situation. You can ask your allies for help with this, and discover some strategies that work for you. You can roleplay to practice using different strategies, so you feel more prepared for a future situation.

Being Aware of My Physical and Emotional Status

Becoming aware of my own physical and emotional status helps me recognize how I am feeling. Once I recognize my feelings, I can learn ways to cope with physical or emotional situations.

STATUS	EXAMPLES	WHAT I CAN DO
Know and name the emotions I am feeling and their intensity	Am I annoyed, angry or furious? Feelings can have low, medium or high intensity.	Learn how to manage intense feelings and calm down.
Know the signs that tell me when my stress level is rising	Is my face getting hot? Do I feel like I am "escalating?" I can tune into signs in my body that suggest I am getting upset.	Learn ways to reduce the stress or calm myself.
Know things that upset me or triggers that set me off	What are the things that change a good day into a bad day? When things are going smoothly, what kinds of things make me "lose it?"	Learn to avoid things that upset me when that is possible, and learn to cope with them when they can't be avoided.

34 • Come to Life! Your Guide to Self-Discovery

STATUS	EXAMPLES	WHAT I CAN DO
Know when I am struggling or need help	Am I stuck on a problem? Do I feel like giving up?	Seek advice or assistance from someone else.
Know when I'm out of balance physically	Do I often feel low on energy or tired? My body sends signals when something's not right. I can learn to read the signals.	Give my body what it needs whether it is food, rest, medical care or something else.
Know when I'm out of balance emotionally	Am I feeling unmotivated, sad, anxious, angry or depressed on a regular basis?	If this is happening, I can recognize it and get help.
Know what sensory things bother me	What sounds, smells or other elements in the environment distract or upset me?	Identifying my sensory stressors can help me avoid or adapt to them. I can let others know what I need to be comfortable.

Chapter Two • 35

Reading Signs and Signals

In addition to understanding yourself and how you respond to the world, you also need to be aware of how other people respond to you. Self-awareness includes noticing how you are fitting into the situation you are in. Noticing how others react to what you do or say is particularly important so you can make adjustments as needed.

For example, a young woman noticed that her classmates groaned each time the teacher called on her. The groaning was a signal that something was not right, so she needed to figure out what was going on. In this case, she waited for a private time to ask a classmate what the issue was.

It turned out that people in the class thought she asked too many questions. They thought her questions went on and on and she was not respecting the teacher's time. The young lady needed to know this so she could adapt to the situation and figure out another way to get her questions answered.

She and the teacher worked out a plan where she would write her questions on sticky notes, and see how many questions were answered during class. She would cross off all the questions that were answered. If any questions were left, she could show them to the teacher after class to get the answers she needed.

This kind of self-awareness is also called *self-monitoring*: being aware of what is going on around you and adjusting or doing something differently, if needed. When you self-monitor, you observe what others are doing and saying. Then you can decide if your behavior is similar and/or appropriate. This helps you adjust what you do or say to make the situation more positive.

An example is having dinner with others in a restaurant. Good manners tell us to wait until everyone has their food before we begin eating. If you did not know this rule, you might start eating as soon as you are served. If you look around and see everyone else waiting, you can put down your fork and knife and wait, too.

This skill is also called *reading context*. Expectations for what to do and say can change, depending on where you are and the people you are with. Being at home with family is a *context* or situation that is usually informal and relaxed, with familiar expectations and rules. Going for jury duty at a courthouse is a completely different context with procedures and social rules that are very different than those at home.

Reading context means you think about the situation or place you are in. Then you decide what social rules apply. You can observe others to see what they're doing. This can help you feel more comfortable and blend in socially.

The infographic *Reading Signs and Signals* sums up this information and can help you learn to *Know Yourself*. Taking the time to explore these ideas creates a strong foundation for our next steps: *Love Yourself* and *Be Yourself*.

Reading Signs and Signals

I need to understand how I respond to the world and how other people respond to me. Self-awareness also means noticing how I fit into different situations. I can also learn to notice how others react to things I do or say.

IDEA	WHAT IT MEANS	BENEFIT TO ME
Self-monitoring	"Reading myself" physically and emotionally to be sure I am OK. Tuning in to my own body and mind to be aware of how I am feeling.	Helps me function at my best, physically and emotionally. Helps me recognize when things are not quite right, so I can take action and make adjustments.
Self-regulation	Taking stock of my physical and emotional status. Identifying "triggers" that upset me and using coping strategies.	I notice when things are not going well, physically or emotionally. I can take action and make adjustments to get back on track.
Social self-monitoring (reading context)	Being aware of what is going on around me. Recognizing the need to adjust, or act differently, especially due to the reactions of others to me.	I observe what others around me are doing and saying. Then I decide if my behavior is similar and/or appropriate. I can adjust if needed.

Activity 2B

Now It's Your Turn

Once you've made a conscious decision to believe in yourself and your ability to influence your own life, you will probably need to do something practical to grow and progress. In addition to *"Who Are You?"* in Activity 2A, here are some more activities that you might like to explore. Your allies can also do these with you to help you learn to become more self-aware and empowered.

Start Small

If tackling a big goal seems too hard, start with a small step in the right direction. For example, maybe your goal is to have more friends. You have to get to know people (make acquaintances) before you have friends.

A good way to get started is being friendlier with people you already know. My mom always encouraged me to be a good friend to my brother Danny and my sister Lisa, practicing my friendship skills at home. Danny and Lisa tell me that they appreciated my efforts. If you don't have brothers or sisters, you can be friendly with people you see regularly like classmates or neighbors.

One friendly thing to do is to give compliments. Look at the person, get their attention, greet them and let them say "hello" back. Then say something positive. Giving compliments is a good way to engage with people and make a good impression. Being friendly helps you open up to people who have something in common with you.

In another example of starting small, I have a friend who wanted to work in a preschool but did not think she could accomplish that goal. Using the "small-steps strategy," she started out babysitting for a short time with an older child. Then, she moved to longer periods with that child. Next, she babysat for a younger child for a short amount of time, then for longer periods. The strategy of proving that she is capable by taking on tasks that she could accomplish successfully really worked for her.

Many "small successes" can add up to feeling more in control of your life and empowered to continue putting energy and effort into it. What is something you can do today that is a small step in the direction you want to go?

Activity 2C

Do or Do Not

Yoda was on to something in *The Empire Strikes Back*, when he said, "Do or do not, there is no try." I have lived by this advice since I first heard it. According to how Yoda and I think about it, "doing" means giving something your total effort and sticking with it until you succeed. "Trying" implies that you are making a partial effort but don't have the same confidence or dedication.

Deciding to just "try," or giving less than your total effort, may be a sign that you think you are going to fail. Believe it or not, thinking you might fail before you do something can actually *increase* your chances of failing. By eliminating "try" from my vocabulary, I gained more willpower and actually found myself getting better at tasks. Furthermore, when I make decisions, I stick by them. When I choose to "do," I devote all of my energy towards my goal.

Can you eliminate *try* from your vocabulary, just for a day, and see if it helps you feel more determined to *do*? You might be surprised by the results and how much more you are truly capable of when you start to *do* and stop using *try* in your life.

Activity 2D

Think Like Goldilocks

A particular feeling can have a certain intensity or strength, ranging from "very mild" to "very strong." You can be a little bit happy, very happy or extremely happy! Besides being able to name your feelings, you also will want to have a way of measuring how strong those feelings are (very mild, mild, normal, strong, very strong). It is a good idea to learn to recognize feelings *in context*, when they are happening.

To learn about the intensity of emotions, it can very helpful to start with something that is visual and concrete: the volume control on a television set. You are probably familiar with the sound bar that shows how loud or soft the volume is. Some TVs even have a numbering system to indicate the level of volume.

Do a demonstration for yourself. Set the volume on your TV very low. When the volume is too soft, it is not possible to hear. Cover your ears and then blast the volume to get a sense of "too loud." Then re-adjust to find the volume that you consider "just right." The analogy of "too little, too much, just right" applies to lots of things in life. For example, our emotions can be too little, too much or just right. It's a good idea to notice this and adjust as needed to be in the "just right" state (*self-regulation*).

There are different tools you can use to learn to recognize and rate the intensity of your feelings. Electronic apps for your Smartphone or tablet may be handy. You may want to explore options like these:

- Google Play and the Apple Store offer options like "Mood Tracker" by T2 that lets you track your feelings *and* connect the feelings to particular events or situations. Once the intensity is recognized, this can be matched to options for coping or adjusting to a "just right" place. This is another example of self-regulation.

Chapter Two • 41

Activity 2D

- "The Mood Meter App" from the Yale University Center for Emotional Intelligence gives you synonyms for different emotions so you can express just how you are feeling. You can track your emotions and notice if there are patterns at different places and times.

Don't forget to learn to rate physical states like pain, too. It's a good idea to learn how to use a pain scale such as those seen in hospitals or medical offices. You can practice rating how much familiar symptoms hurt (e.g., a cut finger, a bad headache or a broken leg).

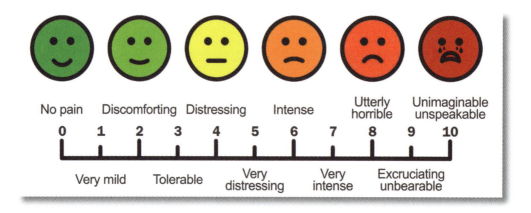

If you do an Internet search (using words like "pain scales" or "pain scales images"), you will get a lot of results. The Wong-Baker FACES Pain Rating Scale uses "smiley face" images to rate pain from "no pain at all" to "the worst pain." The free pain scale from Lucile Packard Children's Hospital uses a lot of words to describe different levels of pain which might be really helpful to understand and describe pain. Source: https://lane.stanford.edu/portals/cvicu/HCP_Neuro_Tab_4/0-10_Pain_Scale.pdf

You can also visit places like Google Play or the Apple Store to see what pain rating apps are available. Many are free. One example is Painometer by Algos which uses drawings of faces to rate pain. Pain Rating Scales by Etz Medical offers different ways to rate pain including a number system and icons.

Activity 2E

Name and Narrate

We talked about *self-regulation* of emotions which means recognizing and managing the feelings you are having. In fact, it's a good idea to learn to recognize feelings when they are happening, or *in context*. One of the best ways to do this is for a parent, teacher or other ally to describe their feelings in an emotional moment and cue you to notice your own feelings. They can start with something as simple as saying, "Wow, I'm really hungry right now, are you?"

Allies can talk about their thoughts and feelings out loud. They can model and describe their own feelings and encourage you to do so for yourself. Once you have the idea, you can switch roles and you can be the one to do the modeling and cue your ally to name their own feelings.

Allies can also help you tune into your internal and physical states by "reading you" in different real-life situations. If they see you are looking tired, they can say, "I see you are kind of slumping in your chair and your eyes are drooping. You look tired. Do you need a nap?" If they see you escalating due to sensory overload, they can point out the physical signs (such as "Do your ears hurt from that loud music?") and suggest a coping strategy ("Let's get out of here!"). They can challenge you to read your own signals, too.

You can turn the table and test out "reading" other people in your life! Tune in to how they might be feeling and any signal you can see in different situations.

Activity 2F

Choose Your Words Wisely

When you become aware of your own physical or emotional states, you can choose words that describe them very accurately. Certain words capture particular feelings and the strength of those feelings very well. Words like *calm*, *annoyed* and *furious* can help you communicate the kind of feelings you are experiencing, along with the level or intensity of the feeling.

You can expand your "feelings" vocabulary through the use of synonyms. Synonyms are different words that mean the same thing or very close to the same thing. For instance, 'hot' and 'warm' are synonyms. 'Cold' and 'chilly' mean almost the same thing. Synonyms are cool because they have hidden meaning built into them. The extra meaning, called *connotation*, is meaning that is suggested or implied.

For example, the words *tasty* and *delicious* can both be used to describe food. If someone says their food is tasty, it means that the person likes it. If someone says their food is delicious, it means that the person *really* likes it!

Allies can help you match words like *happiness*, *delight* and *bliss* to familiar situations as a way to help you express the intensity of your emotional states. For example, I'd say, "I'm *happy* when I hear about a new rollercoaster coming soon, I'm *delighted* when a new ride is about to open at my local theme park, and it is *bliss* when I get to go on the ride with my rollercoaster fan club before it opens to the public."

My choice of words lets others know the intensity of feelings I am having. My choice of words also shows that I am aware of the intensity of my own feelings. Parents and teachers can provide sets of synonyms (like *angry*, *outraged* and *furious*) and ask you to link them to specific past (and current) experiences.

You can also generate your own sets of synonyms for things you are interested in. For instance, for *Star Wars* fans, R2-D2 is *naughty*, Grand Moff Tarkin is *sinister* and Darth Vader is *evil*. Once you expand your synonym vocabulary, you can use those words when you need them. There are apps for synonyms, too, like Synonym by Dua Tech at Google Play or Dictionary.com Dictionary & Thesaurus at iTunes by Dictionary.com, LLC.

Activity 2F (continued)

A Note to Allies

When it comes to exploring emotions with people on the spectrum, it is best to avoid asking, "How would you feel if...?" Many people with ASD have a hard time imagining things they have not experienced themselves. When I was 13 years old, I told my mom, "If it hasn't happened to me, my mind is a blank page."

When people ask about unfamiliar things, it is hard to imagine. The answer to this kind of question is often, "I don't know." Instead, refer to a concrete memory of a real experience by asking, "How did you feel when...?" Once the person can relate to the feelings of a known experience, you can make a link to a new situation or someone else's feelings.

Activity 2G

Systematize and Measure

Using synonyms and connotation creates a system to help you express different feelings or physical states, along with the intensity or amount of feelings. You may also like using a feelings thermometer or pain scale, and find that they are useful tools.

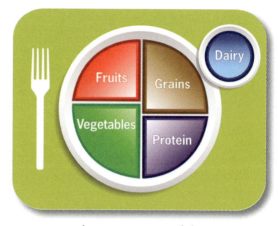

Image courtesy of the U.S. Department of Agriculture.

Another way to help you know your status is to set a standard. Setting a standard means defining certain basic rules, expectations or characteristics. Then you can compare your behavior or other qualities to the standard to see if there is a match or a mismatch.

For example, if someone (like your doctor or parents) says that you should "eat healthy," you may agree that is a good idea. However, you might not know exactly what *eating healthy* means. Just being told to "eat healthy" may be too vague or undefined for you. If you don't have enough information you can't know what foods to choose or how much to eat to "eat healthy."

Instead, it may be helpful to have a concrete, objective way to compare what you eat to specific healthy eating criteria. If someone tells you what foods to eat and how much of a food is a "portion" (serving size or amount to eat), you will have the information you need to make good choices. You can figure out if your food choices measure up as *good*, *better* or *best*.

The U.S. Department of Agriculture's MyPlate is an easy-to-use visual tool for "eating healthy." The free MyPlate program offers specific nutrition information to guide you and measure against (http://www.choosemyplate.gov/MyPlate). This is a great way to compare your food choices to a healthy standard. You can also discover other resources and options for meal planning, nutrition and healthy eating through your doctor, in books and on the Internet.

Once you understand how to create standards, you can systematize just about any aspect of your life!

Activity 2H

Avoid Pink Underwear

Many young people who live at home are used to being taken care of. Some of us don't contribute much to the household. That may be fine for little kids, but teens and adults can do more to help. Sometimes parents end up running your life for you rather than teaching you how to run your own life. This can lead to dependency and *learned helplessness*, a belief that you can't take control of your own life (when really you can!).

The alternative is actively learning how to take on everyday responsibilities. There are many opportunities to learn practical skills. It can feel very empowering to learn how to do the things that need to get done in daily life. Learning life skills can make a real difference in your adult life.

Have you ever worn pink underwear? If something red gets into the wash with white clothes, everything turns pink! Just about everyone makes this mistake at least once. The best way to avoid this is to learn to separate dirty laundry into light and dark colors, and then wash each load separately. Always be on the lookout for those red socks or other items that can sneak into the wrong load.

There is a lot to learn when it comes to taking care of the place you live like cleaning, cooking, washing clothes and paying bills. Take advantage of the opportunity to learn to take care of yourself and your family while living at home or in a transition program. You might find out you actually *like* doing some of these chores and you may get really good at them!

Remember that the people around you have learned a lot from experience and their own mistakes. Your allies have a lot they can teach you. Ask them to teach you what they know. Then, volunteer to help more by asking, "What can I do to help?"

Take on one task at a time until you are really good at it. You may be amazed by your ability to get things done. Besides, your efforts will be appreciated by those who have spent so many years taking care of you. It is great preparation if your goal is to move out of your parents' house and live on your own someday.

Activity 2H

My mom reminded me about the day she taught me how to pay bills. She now realizes she actually went about it all wrong! She brought out the checkbook and all of the bills at once. I was instantly overwhelmed. When she saw my reaction, she cleared the table except for the water bill.

She showed me how to find the amount owed, write a check and fill in the check register. Next, I had to find the right envelope and put the check and bill in the envelope facing the right way, so the address would show through the window. I put the stamp and return address label on the envelope. That is a lot of steps for one bill!

Then we practiced together with the gas bill. I had the hang of it and she watched me pay the trash bill on my own. Once I understood what was expected, I could easily handle one bill at a time. Eventually, I was so comfortable that I could take on all the bills from the bill rack at once with no problem. With bill paying mastered, my mom taught me about money and banking, too.

Now that I live in my own apartment, paying bills is part of the routine of taking care of myself and my home. It took me several years to master the skills I needed. Along the way I found there are many tools available to help me. Apps and Smartphone tools like timers, calendars and organizers can assist us all in doing the tasks we need to do. When it comes to paying bills, online tools like automatic bill payment can make life easier. Ways of doing things can change rapidly, but that is OK! We all adapt and change with the times so that we can become our best selves!

What household chore would you like to learn? You might find some chores are fun, like cooking or baking. You might find out you like to organize your space and your life!

Check out the infographic *Housekeeping Tasks* that shows some of the housekeeping chores people do to take care of the place they live. Today's a great day to get started learning how to do any of these things. Once you learn one, pick another to learn. You will be proud of what you can do!

Activity 2H (continued)

Housekeeping Tasks

I can learn to do chores like these while living at home so when the time comes I'll know how to take care of my own room or place. My family will appreciate the help!

CLEANING	FOOD PREPARATION	MONEY & BUDGETING
Wash clothes	Plan healthy meals	Find source(s) of income
Vacuum and sweep	Cook using a stove or oven	Figure out how much I can spend each week
Wash dishes	Cook using a microwave	Keep track of spending
Clean windows	Follow a recipe	Comparison shop
Make the bed	Shop for food	Banking
Clean the bathroom	Store food safely	Use credit cards responsibly
Care for pets	Pack lunches	Pay bills
Trash and recycle	Safe use of knives	Use ATM machines

Chapter Two • 49

Resources

Websites — There are a lot of interesting resources online that can help you explore the ideas from this chapter. Here are a few suggestions.

- *The Speak Up Guide* from the Center for Human Development at the University of Alaska, Anchorage, offers free worksheets and activities to help you Know Yourself. One can help you identify your strengths, talents, challenges and needs. Other activities cover communication/assertiveness, problem-solving, rights and responsibilities, self-determination, etc.
https://www.uaa.alaska.edu/centerforhumandevelopment/selfdetermination/upload/Speak_Up_Guide.pdf

- Dani DiPirro, designer of positivelypresent.com, offers maps and worksheets to help you discover what is most important to you and how to get there.
https://thegirlwhoknows.com/self-discovery-tools/

- Free self-assessments help determine what kind of personality you have and give you a better idea of your strengths and opportunities for improvement.
http://www.internationalcounselor.org/for-students-their-advisors/free-tools-for-self-discovery

- Learn more about the "Big 5" Personality Traits, which are dimensions of someone's personality. The Very Well website explains what extraversion, agreeableness, openness, conscientiousness, and neuroticism mean and how personality impacts your life at https://www.verywell.com/the-big-five-personality-dimensions-2795422. You might also like the Wikipedia's explanation.
https://en.wikipedia.org/wiki/Big_Five_personality_traits

- The Myers-Briggs company is well known for its' personality tests that help you understand more about your personality in four areas: Directing and Receiving Energy, Taking in Information, Making Decisions and Approaching the Outside World. Psychologists and other support personnel are often trained to give this kind of test, so that is an option you may want to check out. You can also pay a fee to take the *Myers-Briggs Type Indicator®* assessment online, which has 93 questions and takes about 15 minutes to complete.
https://www.mbtionline.com/AbouttheMBTI

Videos — Here are a few suggestions of online videos that can help you explore some of the ideas in this chapter.

- A video featuring motivational speaker Les Brown discusses the importance of realizing you only have one life and why you must live what is in you. If you don't know what is in you, find it or create it.
https://www.youtube.com/watch?v=UQaZRelye40

- Patrick Betdavid, author of *The Life of an Entrepreneur in 90 Seconds*, poses 83 questions in his "ultimate self-discovery questionnaire" to help you begin accepting yourself and your reality.
https://www.youtube.com/watch?v=wA122H9madk

- Jaggi Vasudev, aka "Sadhguru," an Indian yogi, philanthropist and author, discusses getting to know yourself fully and the importance of not compromising yourself by hoping others will make you happy.
https://www.youtube.com/watch?v=al0B8qUkayw

- Internet personality and entrepreneur Gary Vaynerchuk discusses self-awareness by accentuating strengths as well as accepting shortcomings.
https://www.youtube.com/watch?v=j6tKf1IR5j8

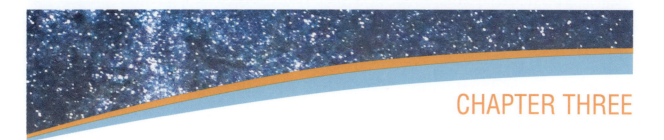

CHAPTER THREE

Love Yourself

Know Yourself. Love Yourself. Be Yourself. In this chapter, we will focus on the second part of this self-discovery process: *Love Yourself.* Loving yourself means acknowledging that you're a unique person who is deserving of your own love and the love of others.

Love yourself means you accept yourself as an imperfect human with both strengths and challenges. *Love yourself* means you know your value and recognize that you have something to contribute to the world. *Love yourself* means you know you have the potential to grow and adapt so you can become your best self.

Love yourself doesn't mean thinking you are better than others. It means you respect yourself and know you are worthy of the respect of others. Loving yourself is a positive thing that can create positive energy in your life.

Accepting That I Have Autism

My journey to "loving myself" included accepting autism as part of me. Learning to love yourself as a person with autism or any kind of disability or learning difference is essential for personal development. Unfortunately, this side of self-awareness is often overlooked for young people in transition to adulthood.

For example, when someone on the autism spectrum is very bright, it is easy to just focus on gifts, talents and abilities. These are definitely something to celebrate! However, focusing only on strengths and pretending that challenges don't exist can be a true disadvantage. It can mean that you might overestimate your abilities (thinking you have more skills than you actually do).

Chapter Three • 53

Focusing only on strengths can overshadow your challenges. When this happens, no one is paying attention to areas where you need help to develop important skills (social, communication, organization, life skills, etc.). When a person's true needs are not recognized, he or she is less likely to get the kind of help needed to be successful.

People with ASD or any other difference often sense that they are different, even from a young age. They want to know *why* and look to their parents for answers. Sometimes parents worry that if they tell the truth, the child will have low self-esteem. As a result, parents don't answer the question truthfully. Sometimes they don't know how to explain it, or the time never seems right.

Whether it is fear of how the child might react or other worries that keep parents from being open with information, the end result may be that the young person is not able to fully understand or accept himself (herself) or his (her) diagnosis.

Not telling the truth about someone's diagnosis can be counter-productive. Not cluing someone in about all their traits (including the challenging ones) can actually hurt self-esteem. Young people may blame themselves for their struggles or failures, rather than understand that certain issues related to the disability are at the root of a problem.

Sometimes parents don't explain a disability to their child or teen because they themselves are in denial about it. Acceptance begins at home and is the key to removing the shame and stigma that are still sometimes associated with disability. Once I knew my parents accepted my autism, it was easier for me to accept my autism.

Understanding and Acceptance

My parents were aware that I was different from other kids, but they waited several years before taking me for a diagnosis. As they learned more about autism, they began to be more open and honest with me. Bit by bit, over time, they shared information about ASD and how it affected me. They were very factual and accepting which, in turn, helped me accept these facts about myself.

In some ways, I was relieved to find out that I had autism! I was aware that I was socially awkward, struggled to make friends and was alone a lot. I knew I repeated lines out of movies and watched certain parts of videos over and over. I wondered why I went to social skills classes but my brother and sister didn't.

Autism explained my differences and it actually made sense to me. In fact, I was relieved to know that there was a reason that some things were so hard for me. I also found relief in knowing that it wasn't my fault and that I wasn't the only one with autism.

My mom had another way of explaining autism to me. She said that autism was "a pattern of differences" with social, behavior, communication and sensory issues. She said that I could get help with those things. There was hope that I could improve and be happier. She also pointed out how many areas of strength I had, and that some of my strengths (persistence, determination, a good memory) could help me overcome my challenges. These realizations helped me accept that I have autism and accept myself. I did not have to be ashamed of my differences.

Yet, even after learning about my diagnosis and how I was affected by ASD, I told my parents, "I don't want to have autism. I want to be like everyone else." This reaction is understandable. Everyone wants to fit in and feel like they belong. I was afraid I couldn't belong if I had autism.

My parents taught me that everyone is different and that it is OK to be different. Children, teens and adults need to know that they are unconditionally loved and accepted, disability included. This gives young people the confidence they need to move forward and make progress in their lives.

It can be a great disadvantage to join the adult world after high school without fully understanding and accepting all aspects of yourself. It can be a definite advantage to be aware of your own quirks, abilities and needs while also feeling comfortable with this knowledge.

It can take time to understand and accept the features of autism (or any other learning difference or disability you may have). If you are struggling with this, you might benefit from some extra emotional support. Many young people need help from counselors or therapists to come to terms with their disability and feel good about who they are. I really benefitted from these services, but know that many people who need them aren't getting them. If you need help, please speak up and ask for it! You can talk to your allies about this and explore options.

Nobody's Perfect

Loving yourself includes self-compassion. Self-compassion means accepting your imperfections and forgiving yourself for not being perfect or getting it right all the time.

Many people on the autism spectrum are very hard on themselves and have perfectionist tendencies. No one is perfect, and no one expects you to be perfect.

Be kind to yourself, rather than being your own worst enemy. Don't beat yourself up when you make a mistake. If you are too hard on yourself, you're more likely to give up when you don't get the results you want right away. Think of a mistake as a learning opportunity. Know you have a chance to do better next time.

If something bad happened in the past, work on letting it go. Dwelling on mistakes can cause anxiety that holds you back. Just like your family and friends love you for who you are and forgive you when you make a mistake, forgiving yourself for not being perfect is part of loving yourself.

Summing It All Up

The infographic *Love Myself* sums up this discussion and can help you learn to love yourself. This step in the journey of self-discovery can prepare you to get in the driver's seat and take your life in the direction you want to go!

Love Myself

I'm a unique person who is deserving of my own love and the love of others. I can accept myself as an imperfect human with both strengths and challenges. Loving myself means I know my value. I recognize that I have something to contribute to the world. I have the potential to grow and change to become my best self.

IDEA	WHAT IT MEANS	BENEFIT TO ME
Self-acceptance	Accepting myself as an imperfect human with both strengths and challenges.	Helps me recognize my potential to grow and change to become my best self.
Self-compassion	Accepting my imperfections. Forgiving myself for not being perfect or getting it right all the time.	Helps me get over feelings of perfectionism and relate to other humans who aren't perfect either. I can be kind to myself, as I would be to anyone else who makes a mistake because they're human.

Now It's Your Turn

Once you have made a conscious decision to love and be kind to yourself, you might like some opportunities to help you grow and progress in that area. Here are some activities that you might like to explore. Your allies can also use some of these ideas to help you learn to love yourself.

Activity 3A Infographic 1: TALENTS

Recognize Your Talents, Skills and Positive Traits

In order to love yourself, it is really important to identify your talents, know what you do well, and recognize positive traits or characteristics about yourself. Here are some simple definitions:

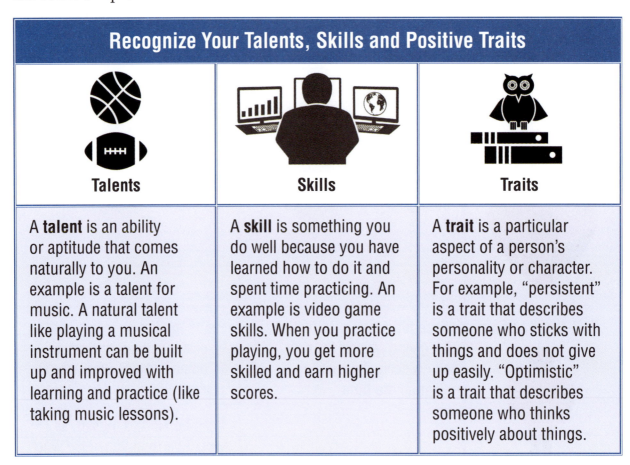

Talents	Skills	Traits
A **talent** is an ability or aptitude that comes naturally to you. An example is a talent for music. A natural talent like playing a musical instrument can be built up and improved with learning and practice (like taking music lessons).	A **skill** is something you do well because you have learned how to do it and spent time practicing. An example is video game skills. When you practice playing, you get more skilled and earn higher scores.	A **trait** is a particular aspect of a person's personality or character. For example, "persistent" is a trait that describes someone who sticks with things and does not give up easily. "Optimistic" is a trait that describes someone who thinks positively about things.

Following are three infographics with examples of talents, skills and traits that people often have (including people on the autism spectrum, or with other disabilities). You may have many of these positive characteristics yourself. The infographics may also help you think of some other positive things about yourself that aren't on the lists.

Recognizing the many positive things you have going for you can help you feel good about yourself and love yourself. It can also help you recognize choices in life that fit you well. After you look over and fill out the three infographics, we will suggest another way to use the information, to help you learn to love yourself.

Activity 3A Infographic 1: TALENTS

Focus on the Positive Areas of Natural Ability: TALENTS

People are born with different gifts and talents. Having a talent means you can do something easily without much teaching. An example is a gift for music: the ability is there. Teaching or lessons can strengthen or enhance a person's natural ability. I can give examples of any of the natural talents I have. I can also add other talents I have that aren't on this list.

Area of Talent or Natural Ability	Icon	Do I Have This Talent? My Example:
Performance: Singing, dancing, playing an instrument, etc.		
Visual Arts: Drawing, painting, photography, multi-media graphic arts, visual arts, cartoons, etc.		
Communication: Expressing ideas through writing, song or other media.		
Repair: Ability to discover why something does not work and fix it so it works again. Examples include watch, car and computer repair.		
Mathematics or Numbers: Using different math operations like addition and multiplication. Examples: Do calculations, use statistics, interpret graphs and tables.		

Chapter Three • 59

Activity 3A Infographic 1: TALENTS (continued)

Area of Talent or Natural Ability	Icon	Do I Have This Talent? My Example:
Manufacture: Ability to put parts together to make a whole. Examples: Putting watches together, working on computer micro-boards.		
Information Technology (IT): Using computers, devices and the Internet for various purposes. Examples: Design web pages or apps, create content, share information or use social media, video games.		
Categorizing: Ability to see order and patterns in our world and the universe. Examples: Grouping things that belong together, sorting materials and using systems to organize things.		
Arranging Objects: Ordering and organizing things. Examples: Setting tables in conference centers or banquet halls, or organizing merchandise in stores, warehouses and order centers.		
People: Interest, desire and ability to help others. Examples: Teaching, childcare, healthcare or beauty service.		
Animals: Care for and interact with animals, including pets, farm animals, zoo animals, etc. Examples: Working in a pet store, a zoo or on a farm; dog or horse grooming.		

60 • Come to Life! Your Guide to Self-Discovery

Activity 3A Infographic 1: TALENTS (continued)

Area of Talent or Natural Ability	Icon	Do I Have This Talent? My Example:
Nature: Having a "green thumb" or a natural ability to grow and care for plants. Examples: Caring for natural resources like forests, or working in a flower shop or as a gardener.	🌳	
Food preparation: Preparing meals, baking or serving food. Examples: Working in a kitchen, restaurant or catering.	🧁	

Other talents:

Chapter Three • 61

Focus on the Positive Things I've Learned to Do: SKILLS

A skill is something I can do well because I have learned how! My skill improves when I spend time practicing. An example is video game skills. When I practice playing, I get more skilled, and earn higher scores.

Here are some examples of skills people might have. It is great to recognize my skills and use them in life! I can give examples of any of the skills I have learned. I can add also add more of my skills to this list.

Area of Skill: Things I Can Do	Do I Have This Skill? My Example:
Share deep knowledge on particular topics	
Remember how to do something once I have done it a few times	
Explain how something is made or how it works	
Compare how something is done and how it should be done	
Stick with a task until it is finished	
Find or remember facts and answers	
Handle repetitive routines or jobs	
Put things where they belong	
Read maps and navigate to different places	
Solve problems	
Other skill	

Activity 3A Infographic 3: TRAITS

Focus on the Positive, My Personality Features or Characteristics: TRAITS

A trait is a particular aspect of my personality or character.
My traits make me a unique and interesting person.
Some traits can work in my favor when I want to reach my goals.
I can check off and give examples of some traits I have.

TRAIT: I am	Do I Have This Trait? My Example:
Kind	
Detail-oriented	
Focused	
Reliable	
Dedicated	
Loyal	
Honest	
Patient	
Gentle	
Willing to learn	
Disciplined	
Other trait	
Other trait	
Other trait	

Chapter Three • 63

Activity 3B

Say It Out Loud

Now that you have more information about your talents, skills and traits, here's an infographic that you can use to identify some of the great things about yourself in each of these areas. Pick five things from each of the three infographics that you really like about yourself, and fill out your *Top Five List*.

Once you have completed your Top Five List, stand in front of a mirror, and say out loud what you love about yourself. Go through each item on the list and say, "I love my _____." This activity helps you recognize and embrace the many reasons to love yourself. It reminds you that you're worthy of your own love and the love of others.

My Top Five List: Things to Love About ME		
TALENTS Abilities in particular areas	**SKILLS** Things I do well	**TRAITS** Positive characteristics
1.	1.	1.
2.	2.	2.
3.	3.	3.
4.	4.	4.
5.	5.	5.

Activity 3C

Give Back

How can you build self-confidence and appreciate your own abilities? By shining in an area of strength while contributing to the good of others or the community. It can feel empowering and energizing to tutor someone in a subject you are strong in (like math), show someone how to do something (like how to give a dog a bath) or be helpful (setting up a new computer system for a relative or neighbor). Volunteering can be especially rewarding if you've never had the chance to use your power to make a difference by helping others.

For example, I was a referee for youth soccer for several years. I knew all the rules and applied them fairly, including when my brother or sister were playing a game. I felt happy when people told me that I was a good ref. I got to know a lot of people in my town, who recognized me away from the game field and greeted me with a friendly smile.

I have also volunteered for over a decade for Safe Rides—a program that gives free rides home to high school students who have been drinking or don't want to ride with a driver who is under the influence of drugs or alcohol. At first I was a dispatcher, then I was a driver, and now I am a trainer and adult supervisor. I love this program because it saves lives. I feel good making a difference. When I am recognized for my service I feel appreciated and more confident in myself.

Many people who are on the spectrum or have other disabilities lead lonely lives, although this is not what they want for themselves. Giving back is not a solitary activity! In addition to sharing something you enjoy with others, service has the added bonus of forming friendships and building relationships.

Hopefully the activities in this chapter helped you have a good idea about some of your skills and talents. How can you put them to good use and help others?

Chapter Three • 65

Activity 3C (continued)

For example, if you love animals, maybe you can volunteer at an animal shelter. If you like to garden, maybe you can cut the grass or plant flowers for a neighbor who can't do those chores anymore. When you make a good match between your interests and abilities you can help make your home, neighborhood or community a better place to live.

There's an added bonus! Doing some kind of community service can help you learn about the kind of work you like and do not like. This can be very helpful when you are ready to plan for a career or figure out what you will do in the future. In some cases, volunteering can even lead to a job offer! All of these things make "giving back" an important step in the process of self-discovery.

You may want to ask your parents, teachers or mentors to help you explore options and figure out how you can contribute and connect. You can visit service websites like Project Human Kindness at https://hellohumankindness.org. You may also want to check out the "Get Involved" section at Youth Service America http://ysa.org/ to learn more about service opportunities.

Resources

Websites—There are a lot of interesting resources online that can help you explore the ideas from this chapter. Here are a few suggestions.

- Author Darin L. Hammond explains what self-love means and identifies 10 Superpowers You Gain as You Learn to Love Yourself.
http://www.lifehack.org/articles/communication/10-superpowers-you-gain-you-learn-love-yourself.html

- Deepak Chopra suggests Seven Ways to Love Yourself Unconditionally that may help with the process of learning to love yourself.
http://www.huffingtonpost.com/2014/04/15/love-yourself-unconditionally-deepak-chopra_n_5120399.html

- Marc Chernoff shares 16 things you can do to love yourself, including showing gratitude and doing something that makes you happy every day.
http://www.marcandangel.com/2015/05/10/16-simple-ways-to-love-yourself-again/

- For young adults (aged 18-40) looking to meet other young adults and make a difference in the world, Junior Chamber International (JCI) connects members to social, professional and volunteer networking opportunities in an effort to better serve humanity.
https://www.jci.cc/

- For those looking to make a difference in the world through volunteer work, this website utilizes volunteer action centers to provide people that want to be at the center of change in world-changing projects.
http://www.pointsoflight.org/handsonnetwork

Videos—Here are a few suggestions of online videos that can help you explore some of the ideas in this chapter.

- Nathaniel Solace, a coach and motivational speaker, created a must-see video about putting yourself first so you can then love others. This video is for you if you enjoy looking at scenes from nature while hearing how you can be a better and more loving person. It can also be calming to look at without the sound on.
  https://www.youtube.com/watch?v=IAQJ2yqfQME

- Cambria Joy, an international fitness expert, shows how to see past your imperfections and love you for you. Whether it is your weight, a skin condition or some other trait you do not like or you think others do not like, this will help build your self-confidence by accepting that you are all right.
  https://www.youtube.com/watch?v=YeBZlTBw9iA

- A video step-by-step checklist on ways to focus on loving yourself to improve your relationships.
  http://www.howcast.com/videos/402270-how-to-love-yourself/

- Transformational life coach and CEO of "Motivating the Masses" Lisa Nichols discusses ways to love yourself and accept your own beauty, both inside and out.
  http://hellobeautiful.com/2014/03/23/tips-on-loving-yourself-more/

- Louise Hay, a motivational author and founder of Hay House, offers ways to increase your self-esteem by focusing on loving yourself so that you can heal your life and become a better person.
  http://www.healyourlife.com/12-ways-you-can-love-yourself-now

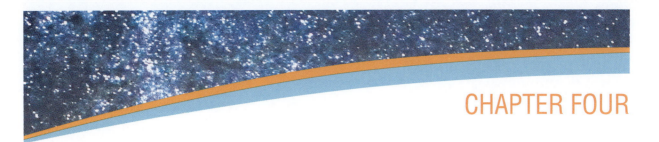

CHAPTER FOUR

Be Yourself

Now we'll talk about the last step in the mantra: *Be Yourself*. Be yourself means being brave enough to adapt and grow in order to become the best version of yourself. Why should you adapt and grow? Because your own effort may ultimately make you the person you want to be *and* enable you to do the things you want to do.

The idea of needing to adapt might be a little sensitive for some people. There are those who say, "I don't need to change; there's nothing wrong with me!" Others say, "I'm fine the way I am; the world needs to adapt to me!" The reality is that everyone, whether they have a disability or not, has to adapt or change a bit to fit into the world. Being open to change means that you are willing to grow and explore new things. It does *not* mean that something is wrong with you.

The key to personal growth is being willing to learn new skills, do new activities and adapt to the world without giving up your true self or core identity. Remember the "Who Am I?" question in *Chapter Two: Know Yourself*? Learning and growing does **NOT** take away from who you are. It gives you new answers to the question, "Who Am I?" When you adapt and grow, you might be able to add answers like, "I am an organized person," "I am a dancer" or "I am a good friend." This can add to the quality of your life.

No one can change you; **you** have to want to change, grow and evolve. Once you decide to change, grow and evolve, you will start to see the results that you want in your life. It starts with believing that you can grow, and accepting that growth is a good thing. This kind of thinking can help motivate you and energize you to become your best self.

Will You Embrace Change?

Let's talk a bit more about embracing change and specifically how it relates to people with ASD. Let's face it: Those of us with autism often have difficulty with change. Adapting to new situations and changing circumstances can be a nightmare. Whether it's getting used to a new activity, navigating a new place like college or settling into a new routine, change can be upsetting and make you feel anxious.

What's worse, sometimes when you finally get the hang of something new, some aspect of it changes. For example, you can get used to a new class in school and then the teacher goes on leave and a substitute takes over for the rest of the year. Or when you learn to do something one way (like drive a certain route to school) and then suddenly have to do it in a different way (maybe because a road is closed for construction).

When change is unexpected, it can feel like the world is coming to an end. Once you have had these kinds of experiences (or even more upsetting ones), the anticipation of being asked to do something new can start an anxiety cycle. When you feel anxious, new tasks can seem even harder.

If you recognize what I am talking about here, you may also know from your own experience that it is common to retreat to your comfort zone when you feel there is a "demand" to change. You may pull back like a turtle going into its shell.

Maybe you stay home or retreat to your room. You may seek out things that are familiar. It can be calming to eat the same foods, watch the same movies, wear the same clothes, play the same games, etc. You may stay in your comfort zone by sticking to activities you already do and socializing with people you already know, rather than going to new places, doing new things and meeting new people.

An unintended result of pulling back into your shell is that you can get stuck. While it is understandable to want life to stay the same and rely on familiar things, stepping outside of your comfort zone may actually help you grow as a person and have a better life. Do not let fear and anxiety hold you back. It is important to recognize if these kinds of feelings are getting in your way. You can ask for help to learn to cope with your emotions so you can move ahead.

Fighting change or hoping it will stop will only eat away at your happiness and well-being. Accepting that change is OK or even desirable is the first step to move forward. When I accepted that change was a part of life and decided to make life's changes work in my favor, I started living the life that I wanted for myself.

Accepting that change was good for me didn't happen overnight. It happened gradually, over time. When I was in junior high school, my mom enrolled me in social skills classes. I felt anxious and didn't want to go because I didn't know what to expect. She asked me, "Do you want to make friends?" and I answered, "Yes." She explained that the class would help me do that.

She was right. I made friends with the other kids in the class and went on to use the skills I learned for the rest of my life. It was very important that my mom made the connection between the class and my own goals. This motivated me to attend. When I realized that the classes would help me get something I wanted, I was willing to make the effort, do the work and learn new things. It helped me do something new that I was afraid of doing. I hope your own willingness to change will also help you get what you want in life.

What Do You Want For Yourself?

Hopefully you have identified many talents and abilities that can help you grow. Through dedication and hard work, you can continue to develop your skills. It can be very helpful to write down some goals for yourself. Focusing on things you want to accomplish can help you feel inspired to do what it takes to succeed.

If you are having a hard time thinking of goals, the infographic *My Goals in Life* can help you think about goals in specific areas. It can help you focus on the future you want for yourself. If you don't have the answers you need, you can come back to this infographic later after reading other sections of the book and discovering more about YOU.

My Goals in Life

Knowing what I want to accomplish can help me succeed. I can start with these goals and change them if I need to.

	1. Work (what kind of job I want to have)
	2. Fun (what I want to do to enjoy myself)
	3. School or education (college, degree program, other training)
	4. Relationships (friends, boyfriend, girlfriend or partner)
	5. Living Arrangements (apartment, house, roommates)
	6. Other Goals

Getting On the Road, Literally

When I was in high school, I really wanted to learn to drive. I felt worried, however, thinking about driving lessons. It was a new experience that I was completely unprepared for. My only experience was as a passenger. I thought that driving could be dangerous. I was afraid I might make a mistake that would hurt me or someone else. I knew about the statistics on collisions and wondered if I might become a statistic myself.

I talked about all this with my mom. She realized that to calm my nerves and help me learn, I needed one-on-one instruction and a second brake pedal in the car. She also realized that it was impossible to predict how long it would take for me to become a good driver.

She literally told the instructor, "The cash register is open, the clock is not ticking, bring him back when he is a safe driver." Thirty lessons later, I passed my driving test on the first attempt! I am very grateful that my parents provided the support I needed to achieve this.

The whole experience helped me have more confidence in myself. I had proof I was capable and could accomplish things, even something that seemed very difficult at first. It was worth the extra effort and time because I love having the freedom to drive any place I want to go and get there safely. That is something I appreciate every day.

The situation also taught me that there is no shame in needing help and extra time to learn something. I learned to accept help when I needed it. I had resisted getting help in the past because I thought that needing help meant I was stupid.

It turns out that no one is good at everything. Everyone needs help with something at some point in their lives. Many people with ASD or other learning differences need more time and more direct teaching to learn something new. Being open to help, getting the help you need and being willing to do the work can make a real difference.

Adapting for Success

I had another "ah-ha" moment when I took a public speaking course in community college. I had to get up in front of the class to talk, which is something just about everyone feels nervous about. This class challenged me to face my fears (in a safe place). Once I managed my fear of public speaking (the number one fear most people have), I realized that I could overcome other fears that were holding me back.

My willingness to change and take charge of my own destiny was reinforced while I was studying accounting in college. I saw all the efforts my classmates were making to develop themselves, personally and professionally. They dressed professionally, joined clubs, networked with others and found internships. I realized that if I wasn't willing to do the same things, I would be left behind and have fewer opportunities.

Have you ever heard the saying "no risk, no reward"? You will not get the job if you don't fill out the application and interview for the position. You will not get a girlfriend if you don't go up to a girl you like and talk to her. You will never move out of your parents' house if you don't learn how to do some of the tasks you need to take care of yourself, or look for another place to live. While it can be hard and feel scary, taking risks can make life more productive, more exciting and more fulfilling. Success means different things to different people: you can be the author of your own success story.

You Deserve the Chance to Discover Yourself

Know Yourself. Love Yourself. Be Yourself. It's what we want for ourselves. Our allies want to help us succeed and achieve, whether we have ASD, other special needs or no special needs. For these reasons, opportunities for self-discovery and personal development should be a priority for all young adults. If you are already an adult but never had the chance to really think through these things, it's not too late!

Activity 4A

Now It's Your Turn

Once you've made a conscious decision to be your best self and embrace change, you will probably want to take steps to grow and progress. Here are some activities that you might like to explore. Your allies can also do these activities with you to help you learn to become more empowered and self-aware.

Put It in Writing

If life came with a rulebook, we would always know what to do. Unfortunately, it doesn't. Sometimes we have to write the book ourselves, or have our allies help us. If you have ever used an instruction sheet to put together a Lego® model, you know how helpful it can be to have instructions in writing (also called using a visual tool).

When I was an intern in the tax department of a large corporation, they did a fantastic job of explaining things to me and making sure I understood procedures and expectations. I took a lot of notes to help me remember what to do. My notes and the coaching helped me do such a good job that I was promoted to Lead Intern, a supervisory position!

I thought about all the things the new group of interns would have to learn. I decided to create a step-by-step guide for the interns that explained how to do their job. As a result, they were more independent and productive, especially because they could refer back to the manual rather than asking questions. In fact, the guide enabled them to complete the tax filing process faster and more accurately than ever before.

When it comes to being more independent and learning skills for adult life, what do you need a manual to do? Any topic or procedure can be spelled out in writing. You can even use numbered steps and pictures. This kind of visual tool can be a great source of support.

Whether it is learning how to change a flat tire or making mac 'n' cheese, knowing the steps can help you feel better prepared and less anxious when faced with a task or challenge. The infographic *Put It In Writing* can help you identify a few things you would like to learn to do. Then you can decide how to make the task easier with written instructions or another kind of visual tool (diagram, checklist, chart, etc.).

Chapter Four • 75

Activity 4A (continued)

Put It In Writing

Sometimes it is helpful to have a "how-to" guide or written instructions how to do something. I would like to have written instructions or a visual tool to help me do these things:

The next step is picking a few of the ideas you listed and creating your own "how to" tool!

- Choose whatever tool you like that can spell things out, cover all the steps and help you remember. Think of a tool like a cookbook recipe or a set of Lego® instructions, or anything in between. You might like charts, checklists, other visuals or even an app. You can explore options with your allies.

- When putting together a "how-to" guide for situations that involve other people, it can be a good idea to include any "invisible rules" that may come into play. These are social rules that pretty much everyone else knows and follows, that may have to be spelled out for people on the spectrum. Two examples for students are, "Don't make comments about your classmates' physical appearance" and "Don't correct your teacher or professor during class." Including these kinds of reminders in your written instruction or visual tool can be very helpful in new situations. Be sure to talk with your allies to get started to "put it in writing."

Activity 4B

Be Prepared

Part of the fear factor around change is "the unknown." Sometimes when I was asked to do something new, I felt like I was being dropped into a swimming pool without any swimming lessons. Some people compare the situation to being dropped into the middle of a game and told "Go!" without anyone explaining what the game is, how to play or what the rules are.

Preparation for change can be an antidote to this fear of unfamiliar situations. We need someone or something to explain how things work, and what is expected of us in practical matters of daily life.

When it comes to getting helpful information, peer mentoring can be an excellent option. This means asking people your own age what an experience is like (driving, going to college, etc.) or how they handle certain situations (dating, apologizing to someone, etc.). They can share information from their own life. As long as a peer is reliable and trustworthy, asking an "expert" your own age for advice on certain topics (dating, social expectations, etc.) might be better than asking an adult.

I mentioned that when I wanted to get a girlfriend, I went to my sister for advice. I asked her what she looked for in a boyfriend so I had a better chance of being appealing to girls my age. Besides telling me the qualities she liked in her boyfriends (kind, fun, funny, etc.), she let me know that I needed to have friends who are girls before I could have a girlfriend. Girls like to take time to get to know someone before they decide to be a couple.

Can you remember a time when being properly prepared really helped you out? Can you remember a situation that was stressful because you were not prepared? What events or situations in your future are coming up that you want some help to prepare for?

Everyone likes to feel prepared. People like me who have autism may have an even greater need to anticipate and prepare for change. We need "orientation" to new experiences.

Chapter Four • 77

Activity 4B (continued)

One of my employers had an excellent introduction period that explained everything I was expected to do *and* showed me how to **do** it before I started the job. This kind of preparation and the support of a mentor helped me feel more comfortable and confident. I also knew that I was not alone, that I was not the only one having the new experience, and that people were available to help if I needed it.

Are there new activities or experiences that will be happening in your life in the near future? For example, are you going to do job shadowing but are not sure what that experience is like? Are you going to a new place you have never visited before? Do you need more information about a situation or event that is coming up? The infographic *Be Prepared* helps you organize information about these things. Talk with your parents, teachers or other allies if you need help to identify upcoming situations and discuss steps to help you be prepared for them.

Be Prepared

I will be having new experiences and doing new activities in the near future. It would be helpful to be prepared for these things so I know what to expect:

Activity 4C

Identify Options for Support

Another difficulty related to change is feeling like you are being pushed beyond your limits. Instead of feeling excited or happy about a new opportunity (like going to college), you might feel a sense of dread or overload. While preparation can help, you also need to know what kind of help is available in a new situation or place.

In fact, you need to know what services or supports are available and the steps to get them *before* you need them. I've found that before starting something new, it is wise to ask and answer the questions, "What kind of help can I get?" and "Who can help me?"

For example, when I was in college, I needed help writing long papers. Before the semester started, the transition specialist who was working with me told me about a study lab where any student could go who needed assistance with academics. I went there, introduced myself and found out what hours the lab was open.

When the time came to write a paper, I felt better when starting to write knowing that help was there if I needed it. I also felt comfortable when I needed to go to the lab because I was familiar with the place and the staff. They also told me about other resources, such as academic tutoring, that I could use if I needed.

Taking the time to find answers and having things/people ready for when you need them is a better option than struggling to do things alone, or looking for help when you are in "crisis mode." Since it is sometimes hard to warm up to new people, it is helpful to meet people and get to know them when you are calm. In fact, knowing that help is there if you need it can help you feel less anxious and maybe even avoid a crisis.

Activity 4C (continued)

You can use the infographic *Identify Options for Support* to think though situations when you want to be prepared. You can use it to practice or you can use it any time you need to figure this out. We filled in the first row as an example.

Identify Options for Support

I need to know what services or supports are available and how to get them before I need them. Before starting something new, it is a good idea to ask and answer the questions, "What kind of help can I get?" and "Who can help me?" I can fill out this infographic to help me think about new things happening in my own life. Then, I can identify people who can help me.

What is a situation I want to be ready for?	What can help me (tools, services, supports, etc.)?	Who can help me?	What do I need to do to get started?
Writing long papers in college	The writing lab on campus	The tutors in the lab	Look online for the phone number and call for an appointment

80 • Come to Life! Your Guide to Self-Discovery

Activity 4D

How Much Help Would Help?

There are seven areas or *domains* to think about when you are planning for your life in the future: communicating, learning, taking care of yourself, going places in the community, making decisions, independent living, and finances (money). This activity explains more about each of these things.

You can use the infographic *How Much Help Would Help?* to think about how independent you are in each domain today, and how much help you might need in the future. If you are not sure about your answers, you might want to fill out the infographic with someone who knows you well (one or more of your allies).

Directions:

1. Read about each area of adult life. Look at the meaning and examples for each domain.

2. Are you able to do the kinds of activities listed on your own, or do you need help with them?

3. Check off the box that best describes your situation: "I don't need much help with this," "I could use some help with this," or "I need a lot of help with this."

Once you have identified areas where you need help, your allies can help you identify certain skills to build. Then you can decide what skills to work on first, and figure out who can help you learn them. If any of the seven domains seem like they will be a big challenge, you can talk with your allies about the kind of help or services you may need to be successful in life after high school.

Chapter Four • 81

Activity 4D (continued)

How Much Help Would Help?

1. Read about each area of adult life and check out the examples.
2. Decide if I can do these kinds of things on my own, or if I need help.
3. Check the box that best describes how much help I need.
4. Prioritize skills to work on and get started with the first one.

Area of Adult Life	What This Means	I don't need much help with this	I could use some help with this	I need a lot of help with this
Learning	Continuing my education by doing things like: • Taking classes for adults • Getting training • Going to college, etc.			
Self Care	Taking care of myself including: • Physical and mental health • Diet and exercise • Grooming, dressing, etc.			
Self-direction	Having control in decisions about me and my future: • Letting others know what I like, want and need • Thinking things through to make good choices			

82 • Come to Life! Your Guide to Self-Discovery

Activity 4D (continued)

Area of Adult Life	What This Means	I don't need much help with this	I could use some help with this	I need a lot of help with this
Mobility	Having a way to go places in the community by: • Bus, subway or train • Driving • Arranging transit or rideshare			
Independent living	Managing daily life and tasks: • Cleaning and organizing • Planning meals, shopping for food, cooking, etc.			
Economic sufficiency	Having enough money to live on and: • Budgeting my expenses • Paying bills on time, etc. • Banking			

Activity 4E

Find Ways to Cope with Stress and Anxiety

Despite all kinds of planning and preparation, stress and anxiety can't always be avoided. Anxiety can make it very hard to do what you need to do. Past difficulties or failures can create a vicious cycle of doubt that can be like a self-fulfilling prophecy (you predict your own failure and then it happens). When something goes wrong, instead of dwelling on the negative, tell yourself that you can take control of the situation and do things differently next time to get a better outcome.

For example, just about everyone is stressed about taking tests. Past failure can make anxiety leap to new heights. When I was taking the exams to become a CPA, I failed the *Audit* section of the exam twice. I had a lot riding on the test…if I couldn't pass it, I couldn't become a CPA. The situation made me very anxious. Instead of giving in to the stress, I had to muster up the courage to take the *Audit* section again.

The key to taking control of the situation was figuring out what I could do to prepare better. I decided to memorize the *Standard Unqualified Audit Opinion* report word-for-word. This process helped me understand the principles of auditing. I went in for the third attempt believing that this time would be different and it was…I PASSED!!! By changing my approach to the challenge, I succeeded and got the results that I wanted. Hopefully, this type of strategy will help you tackle your own challenges, too.

Think about some challenges you have successfully overcome in the past. Remember a time where you relied on your own grit, determination and hard work to overcome an obstacle. Confidence can be an antidote to anxiety. Remember… you are probably more capable than you think.

Also remember that anxiety affects the mind and the body. Take some time to find some ways to soothe yourself with relaxation, exercise, healthy eating and other coping strategies as shown in the infographic *Find Ways to Cope with Stress and Anxiety*. You'll want some strategies that you can use any time (like deep breathing or counting to ten) as well as daily routines that help you regain calm feelings.

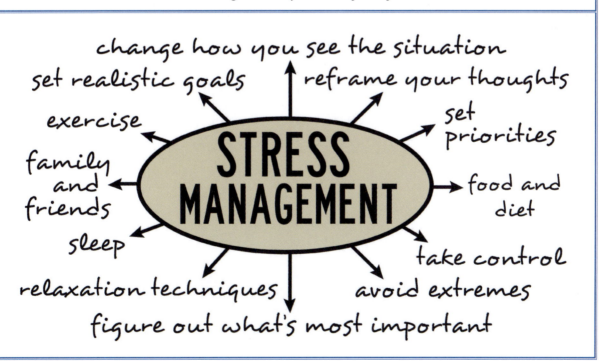

Find Ways to Cope with Stress and Anxiety

I can learn more about options for coping with stress and anxiety. When I find what works for me, I can make "stress management" part of my daily routine.

Resources

Websites — There are a lot of interesting resources online that can help you explore the ideas from this chapter. Here are a few suggestions.

- This self-improvement website offers tools and strategies for how to reinvent yourself and make yourself better every day.
  http://www.theemotionmachine.com/how-to-bring-out-your-best-self

- This blog offers four key principles to becoming happier and more productive in your life.
  http://blogs.psychcentral.com/best-self/2014/08/4-agreements-that-will-help-you-be-your-best-self/

- Best-selling author Dave Kerpen shares ideas about how to become your best self to become a more productive employee or increase your chances of being hired.
  https://www.linkedin.com/pulse/4-simple-steps-becoming-your-best-self-work-dave-kerpen

- This website offers a page to help you reflect on what can be learned from past failures.
  https://www.greatnessmagnified.com/being-your-best-self

Videos — Here are a few suggestions of online videos that can help you further explore the ideas from this chapter.

- A slideshow of motivational quotes with narration.
  https://www.youtube.com/watch?v=GYuc04rQVa4

- Hypnotherapist Abi Levine discusses becoming your best self.
  https://www.youtube.com/watch?v=WlmS_IwTJEs

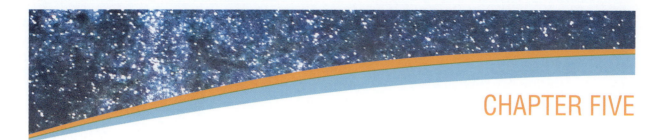

CHAPTER FIVE

Find Yourself

As we get older, we have to make many decisions about our future. Everyone agrees that young people need to have a voice and a say in decisions that affect us. Parents, teachers, counselors and other adults in our lives are waiting to hear what we think and what we want so they can make plans with us.

The problem is that sometimes we can't tell people what we want because we simply do not know! We do not have the answers to important questions such as, "What do I want out of life?", "What job do I want to do?" or "Where do I want to live?" We need to explore these kinds of important questions and find some answers so we can head in the right direction. When we have a better idea of what we want out of life, we have a better chance of achieving our goals.

Being unsure about the future is a common problem for students leaving high school. For those that go to college, thousands of students start college with an "undeclared major" because they have no idea what they want to do in life. While making decisions about their path in life is tough for anyone, it might be even harder for teens and young adults with disabilities.

If you don't plan to go to college, maybe you have other unanswered questions about the kind of work you want to do, where you would live if you move out of your parents' house, and how you would pay the rent. It is hard to plan for our future after high school when we don't have the answers to life's important questions.

The Right Fit

As we discussed in the previous chapters, self-discovery can help you become aware of your strengths, needs, likes and dislikes. Self-discovery also helps you recognize your feelings, motivations and goals. The process of self-discovery can also help you begin to answer the important questions about the future and figure out what is best for you.

Cinderella's slipper is a good analogy about being patient while you search out things that are the right fit for you. Do you remember the fairy tale, when the Grand Duke was assigned the tiring task of going door-to-door throughout the kingdom, searching for the woman whose foot fit inside the glass slipper? He had to be very patient and determined to stick with it until he was successful. Getting the right fit made all the difference in that story! It can take time and persistence to find whatever you are looking for, whether it is a relationship, a place to belong, or a job. During your search, you will learn a lot about yourself and life in general.

Experience is the Best Teacher

It is very helpful to learn about different options when you want to figure out what is best for you. Whenever possible, experiencing options is far better than just knowing about them. World-famous autism expert Temple Grandin says, "The most important thing people did for me was to expose me to new things" (Raymond, 2010). I agree.

For example, when it comes to choosing a career, if you have not been exposed to different job options, you probably do not know what kinds of jobs are available. A chance to see and experience things for yourself is a great way to understand what it means to have a certain job or what it feels like to do the work.

88 • Come to Life! Your Guide to Self-Discovery

Similarly, when it comes to living arrangements, many of us have no idea what it would be like to live in a college dorm, an apartment, share a house with people our age, etc. We can't make good decisions about things if we don't have enough information. Getting the chance to explore options for living is critical in making good choices.

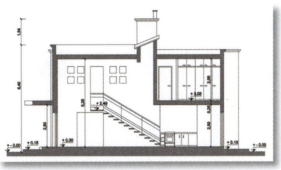

If you want to continue your education after high school, options include online classes, technical school, job training courses, on-the-job training, community college, and university. How can you know which type is best for you if you do not know what each of those options involves? Getting informed and even seeing the options for yourself can help you know what is really right for you.

Sometimes when you need to make a decision, there are too many options and it can feel overwhelming. This chapter is about learning to narrow down the options and make choices that are right for you.

Find Your Niche

Once we understand more about ourselves, we need to find our *niche*. Niche is pronounced *'nitch'* or *'neesh'*. It's a French word that refers to a little space carved into a wall that holds a statue that fits there perfectly. When people say, "Find your niche," it means discover a place or situation where you fit very well whether it is a job, a living situation or a relationship.

e^3 = Explore. Experience. Evolve.

I like math formulas, so I came up with a formula for finding your niche: explore, experience and evolve, or e^3. When you say e^3 out loud, "e to the third power," it gives you a hint about how empowering it can be to explore, experience and evolve. I believe that e^3 is a method that can help you discover what you want for yourself and make decisions that will improve your quality of life.

Exploring different real-life situations and experimenting (or testing things out) helps you grow and change, or evolve. You can learn more about yourself and what is right for you. The e^3 process can help you get the information you need to make choices that are right for you.

The Color of Choice

Let's start with an analogy to explain e^3. Let's say your room is tan and you want to paint it a different color. But where to begin? There are so many colors to choose from! There are primary colors (red, blue, yellow). There are secondary colors (purple, orange, green). Add neutrals (colors not in the rainbow) to the mix and you may find it is really hard to pick from so many choices.

Let's say you like the color blue the best. That's a great step to narrowing things down, but wait! Next, you need to go the paint store to explore "blue" options. The color blue can range from the lightest sky blue to the darkest navy blue and everything in between.

Fortunately, there are samples of paint color at the store called paint chips. They are little pieces of cardboard with every color imaginable. Each color has a name and a number. When you are at the paint store, one strategy for choosing a color is to step back and look at all the chips on the wall from a distance. You can notice if any particular colors grab your attention.

Paint chips are free. Move in closer to look at the chips, and take some home with you. The idea is to see what colors appeal to you the most in the space you will be painting. You can see which color works best with other things in the room like a bedspread or carpet. Figuring out how the color works in the place it will be used (also known as *in context*) can help you narrow down the options. Making a decision in context helps you eliminate some choices and focus in on others.

When you have narrowed things down to four or five of your favorite chips, you can go back to the store to get actual color samples. Samples are tiny cans of paint you can take home and paint right onto your wall. Most people paint a patch of each sample, about 12 inches by 12 inches, and let it dry.

Once the colors are on the wall, you look at them at different times of the day (morning, afternoon, evening). You look at each color with sunlight and lamplight to be sure it appeals to you under all conditions. When you do this, one color should stand out as the one you like best.

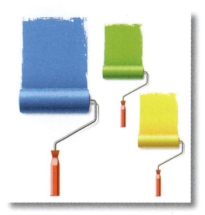

Sometimes in the process, you discover that a color you thought you would love did not really look good in your room. At other times, a color that was just a "maybe" becomes the surprising favorite. Your opinion can change or evolve based on the experiment. This is a very informed way to pick a color. It can help you feel more confident going back to the store to order paint by the gallon.

Of course, before you can transform your room with the color of choice, you have to equip yourself to paint. You have to have the right tools for the job including rollers, brushes, trays, plastic to protect floors and furniture as well as tape to paint straight edges. You have to learn how to paint properly or the whole project can turn into a mess!

One option for learning to paint is watching videos. You can also ask someone who knows how to paint to show you how to do it. Hopefully, after you paint the whole room, you'll be happy with the result. If not, you can always pick again and repaint.

Chapter Five • 91

Connecting to e³

Do you see e³ in this analogy? You explored color options. You listened to the perspectives of others. You sampled options *in context*. You eliminated some options and narrowed down the choices.

Through experience and experimenting, you got enough information to make an informed decision. Your preferences may have evolved or changed in the process. Here are three infographics that illustrate the process of explore, experience and evolve.

e³: Explore. Experience. Evolve.
The Color of Choice: Explore
<ul><li>Every color is an option.</li><li>Narrow down to a favorite rainbow color.</li><li>Consider the full range of tints and shades within the color.</li></ul>
The Color of Choice: Experience
<ul><li>Pick a few of your favorite options.</li><li>Take home the paint chips to see how the color works in the place where it will be used.</li><li>See how the color works with other things in the room (especially things you don't want to change like carpet, furniture and bedding).</li><li>Experiment. Buy samples of a few colors you like and test them out at home.</li><li>Paint patches of each color sample on a wall.</li><li>Look at the color samples on the walls at different times of the day.</li><li>Decide if you are happy with a particular option all day long or if different lighting affects your opinion.</li></ul>
The Color of Choice: Evolve
<ul><li>Pick a color. Make the choice you think is best for you.</li><li>Equip yourself to paint.</li><li>Get painting!</li><li>If the color is not right, you can always repaint.</li></ul>

Apply e³ to Your Life

This color analogy applies to life, too. The e³ process can be applied to many decisions in life. Explore, experience and evolve can apply to dating or picking a college. It can apply to tasting new foods, choosing an apartment or buying a car. Remember that it's OK to change your mind about what you want as you get new information and learn more about yourself. Expect to change or reshape your plans and preferences over time, as you evolve.

The e³ process can help you answer the questions about what you like and do not like, what you want and do not want, what is easy and what is too hard, and what is interesting or boring. It can help you learn about the kind of work you might want to do, or explore places that feel comfortable to be in.

My e³ Work Experiences

I'd like to share the story of how I explored, experienced and evolved by having different jobs during high school and college. When I was in high school, my special education transition team knew that I was a huge movie fan. I knew tons of movie trivia and had memorized the entire dialogue of dozens of films. I was pretty sure I wanted a job in the movie industry. With that goal in mind, the team helped me find several part-time jobs that gave me the chance to explore different kinds of work related to movies, get experience and see where things went from there.

My first paid work experience was at a video store (yes, this was a few years ago!). I restocked videos that customers returned, putting them back on the shelves in alphabetical order. Near the end of my work experience, my mom visited the store. She was upset to find out that I still was re-shelving videos after about four months on the job. She asked the store manager, "Why?"

He said that all the people who were part of the "special education work program" restocked shelves. Because I was part of the program, he assumed I was not capable of doing more than that. He admitted that he did not teach me anything else like operating the cash register, scheduling employees or receiving inventory shipments. He assumed I could not learn those things due to my disability.

Here are some of the lessons my transition team and I learned and took into account when looking for my next job opportunities:

1. Presume competence. I couldn't learn new skills if no one taught me because they didn't believe I could learn.

2. Don't limit opportunities to entry-level experiences. I didn't have opportunities to grow within the store or company when I could have if given the chance.

3. Parents and teachers should regularly check in to see how things are going and make adjustments if needed. I did not realize that my manager was underestimating what I could do; my team did not it know either.

4. I needed better supervision and monitoring from my team, and someone to speak up for me, because I was not able to advocate for myself yet.

Here's my e^3 analysis of that job.

\multicolumn{2}{c|}{My e^3 Example: Job 1}	
Explore	Working in retail.
Experience	Customer interaction, having a boss, being on time to work.
Evolve	I liked earning my own money and spending it how I wanted. I was bored doing the same thing over and over. I wanted more responsibility. I wanted to use talents like my mathematical abilities and learn to run the cash register.

My next job was as an employee at a different video store. I was taught to run the cash register, check movies in and out, do inventory of food and drinks, engage with customers about promotions and boost sales. I mastered these tasks.

Problems came up when I had to help customers who were angry about a store policy. Basically, the store had no more late fees, but customers who brought back a video after a week were charged the full price for the movie. They owned it. Many customers did not understand the policy. When they discovered a charge on their credit card statement, they were very angry. I was often the first person they confronted when they came in the store to complain.

I felt upset and frustrated. I understood why customers were angry, but I was powerless to change the policy. Before the policy was implemented, I had told my manager that it was a terrible idea and that it was going to hurt the business.

It was rough to be on the receiving end of all that anger, especially when it wasn't my fault. I was very anxious and felt like I was at a breaking point.

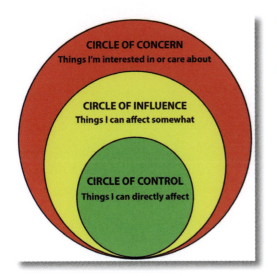

My mom taught me about the circle of concern (things I care about) compared to the circle of control (things I can affect or change). I understood that I was supposed to let go of things I couldn't control (like corporate policy), but that was not easy for me. I was still very upset and felt nervous each time I went to work.

With my mom's help explaining the situation, my supervisor agreed that I would not have to interact with angry customers anymore. Instead, the manager on duty would step in. This was an accommodation for social and communication aspects of my autism. Yet, I found that the situation was still making me miserable. My family and I realized that this job was not the right fit for me, and I quit.

Here's my e^3 analysis of that job.

My e^3 Example: Job 2	
Explore	Different roles in retail, being part of a sales team, learning to run the register, attending team meetings, taking inventory, working at other store locations in the district when needed.
Experience	Dealing with irate customers, learning about circle of concern vs. circle of control, getting an accommodation.
Evolve	Dealing with customer complaints was not the right fit for me. I want to be able to give feedback to the company and have a voice, rather than feeling powerless and shut out.

Next, I went to work in the concession stand at a movie theatre (still looking for the right job that fit with my interest in movies). All employees who ran the cash register were supposed to ask customers, "Would you like to buy the popcorn-drink-candy combo?" I asked every single customer consistently, and it paid off—I won several awards for selling  the most popcorn-drink-candy combos. I also learned how to do food-related jobs, including making popcorn and cleaning the popcorn machine. Once in a while, I got to work in the box office selling tickets. I really loved that!

In this experience, the greatest challenge was other employees. The concession stand was not very well supervised. A lot of my fellow employees goofed off and played pranks. In fact, I was on the receiving end of several pranks, one that was actually harassment. As a result, I did not feel safe working there. My mom and I met with the manager to explain the problem. I did not believe that the bullying would stop, so I left.

Here's my e^3 analysis of that job.

My e^3 Example: Job 3	
Explore	Working in food service in a movie-themed environment, being part of a sales team, using a card-scanning system to track hours worked.
Experience	Selling food and drinks, preparing food items, encouraging customers to upgrade to combos, cleaning (popcorn machine, mopping the floor).
Evolve	I didn't like the informal management style or inconsistent enforcement of policies. I didn't feel like I fit in or was respected by peers. I didn't get to work in the box office very often or learn management skills, like I hoped to. I wanted more room for growth. I realized what I liked best about work was counting the money, an interest that eventually led me to my career in accounting!

Whether positive or negative, you can learn a lot from work experience. Experience helps you answer questions about what you like and don't like, what you want and don't want, what is easy and what is too hard, and what is interesting or boring. It helps you learn about the kind of work environment that feels comfortable to you, and even how values or policies of the company fit (or don't fit) with you. When it comes to career exploration, it's a good idea to be flexible about what kinds of jobs you're willing to do, and persist until you find the right place or duties.

In my case, having different opportunities for exploration and experience helped me grow, adjust and even reinvent myself. I moved from thinking I wanted a movie-related career to realizing that my strength was in mathematics. With more exploration and experience, I ended up choosing accounting because it seemed to match my interests, skills and values. My new dream was to be an accountant for George Lucas because of my love for movies…and *Star Wars* in particular! (In an indirect way that happened, but that's an interesting story for another day.)

Maybe you have a really high goal for yourself, one that few people on earth can achieve like becoming a movie director, developer of the world's best-selling video game, astronaut, etc. I hope you can be one of those people. But let's face it, not everyone can do those things. Therefore, finding a job that is the right fit probably needs to include learning about other jobs in your area of interest.

Take some time to actively discover more about job options that could be a good match for you. Find out how to get paid work or volunteer experiences that can help you evolve. This is an area where your allies can be very helpful, especially if you let them know that is what you want to do!

Your e³ Experience

Have you had the chance to explore, experience and evolve? You can use the following infographic to tell your own story. You can also use it as a guide to begin your e³ journey.

My e³ Example	
Explore	
Experience	
Evolve	

Evolve Using Pro and Con Lists

When you have a lot of decisions to make, a pro and con list can be a really helpful tool. It can help you discover if there are more positive things or negative things involved in a decision. Too many negatives, or "cons," are the sign of a bad fit.

For example, I recently decided to be a freelance driver and pick up passengers who contacted me via a Smartphone app. Here's what I learned after 30 days of exploration and experience.

e³: Explore. Experience. Evolve. Tom's Pro and Con List for Being a Freelance Driver	

PROs (positives)	**CONs (negatives)**
Pick my own hours.	Need to work 8-12 hours per day and 40 hours per week to get the best pay rate.
Make money.	High cost of gas, insurance and maintenance.
Meet interesting people.	Not everyone is a well-behaved passenger.
Work in my own familiar car.	Wear and tear on car, putting on a lot of mileage.
Have the option to make extra money at peak times.	Peak times often mean being up all night (9 p.m. to 4 a.m. shifts).
I am my own boss.	Company policies, such as pay cuts during slow season, are out of my control.

Bottom line? For me, the negatives outweighed the positives. Mathematically, the costs of being a freelance driver in a suburban area meant that it was not worthwhile for me, especially as a full-time job. So I decided to discontinue the work, but I am not sorry I had the experience because I learned a lot about myself…and I have evolved again!

Here's a pro and con list you can use for decision-making:

My Pro and Con List for Decision-Making	
PROs (positives)	**CONs (negatives)**

Finding Answers

It's important to know that there can be many bumps in the road as you work towards finding your niche. Do not expect things to go smoothly all the time. That is real life.

I am not ashamed of the fact that when I started working, I quit several jobs. They were not the right fit for me and they were never going to be. I said, "Thank you for the opportunity," and held my head high as I left. I am fortunate to have had many experiences, good and bad, because they taught me lessons that I carry with me into future jobs. They have helped me become the person I am today.

Now It's Your Turn

Even though you want to expand your horizons, you may not feel ready for new experiences. Unfamiliar things can be scary. Here are some fun ways to explore options and make decisions. You can discover how your preferences can lead to specific choices. You can apply this understanding to real choices you have to make in life. Your allies can help you follow up on these activities and learn more about jobs or other choices that may be right for you.

What's Right for Me?

Coming back to the point where we started, everyone agrees that young people need to have a voice and a say in decisions about their future. Each of us has to discover the answers to important questions.

You never know what job, school, apartment or other choice might be a good fit for you. It can take lot of trial and error to find it. That's why it's a good idea to explore and experience different things. Using the e^3 process (or some other method you like) to find your *niche* is worth the time and effort because it can help you answer the important questions needed to create the future you want.

You can use the infographic *What's Right for Me?* to organize the answers to life's important questions as you discover them. It is fine to change your mind as you learn and grow, so keep updating it! You can also add any other questions about your future that you want.

This may be a good activity to do with your allies, so they can help you go in the direction you want for yourself. Many of the resources listed at the end of this chapter can help you find some of the answers you are looking for. The *Occupational Outlook Handbook*, O*NET OnLine, and the U.S. Bureau of Labor Statistics websites are particularly useful to help you with this infographic.

Activity 5A

<td colspan="3" align="center">**What's Right for Me?**</td>		
<td colspan="3"></td>		
	What makes me happy?	
	What activity do I spend most of my time doing?	
	What do I hope to be doing 2, 5 or 10 years from now?	
	How can I turn my interests into a job?	
	What are some job options in my area of interest?	

102 • Come to Life! Your Guide to Self-Discovery

Activity 5A

	How can I find out what it is like to work in that field?	
	What are some of the skills I have for this job?	
	What other skills do I need for this job?	
	What kind of schooling, education or training do I need?	
	What are the steps to get the job I want?	
	What other questions do I have?	

Chapter Five • 103

Activity 5B

Whose Side Are You On?

If you are a *Star Wars* fan, you might have fun finding out what your *Star Wars* job would be.

1. Visit http://www.playbuzz.com/jonb10/what-would-be-your-star-wars-job

2. Follow the prompts to make the selections that will help the program find the right job for you (your *Star Wars* niche!). Choose your team, transport, weapon, droid and allies. Decide if you will go solo or be part of a team, what your mission/goal will be, etc.

3. Check your results. Do you agree with the choice of *Star Wars* job? Why or why not?

4. Now do the activity again. This time, change preferences to see how the outcome changes.

5. Do you agree with the new choice of *Star Wars* job? Why or why not?

6. What else did you learn from doing this activity?

7. How is this process like making real choices about your life?

Activity 5C

Puppy Love

If you were going to get a dog, what kind of dog (breed) would be best for you? We have an activity and an infographic to help you figure it out!

1. Have fun at the American Kennel Club website to "find a match" and see the dog breeds that could be right for you. Visit http://www.akc.org/find-a-match/#slide1.

2. You'll be asked to select certain preferences for the pet, like noise level, size and where you would be living with the animal.

3. Look at the results. Check out the five breeds that might be a good match for you. Narrow those down to the three that could be the best choice for you. Write these three breed names down on the infographic below.

4. Now look at the trainability, grooming needs and activity level of your three top choices. Do you like traits for each breed? Are there any traits you can't live with that would be a deal breaker and eliminate that particular dog as an option? (Examples include too much barking, shedding, health problems, or cost to buy this kind of dog. Add this information to the infographic under "deal breakers.")

5. Based on your exploration, which breed seems to be the best choice for you?

6. What else did you learn from doing this activity?

7. How is this process like making other choices about your life?

Activity 5C

Puppy Love

I am not really going to get a dog, but learning about different breeds of dogs and figuring out what kind of dog would be the best pet for me is good practice for decision-making.

Instructions:
1. Visit the American Kennel Club website (http://www.akc.org/find-a-match/#slide1) to "find a match" and see the dog breeds that could be right for me.
2. Write down three breed names of dogs that appeal to me on this infographic.
3. Look at the trainability, grooming needs and activity level of my three top choices. Do I like the traits for each breed?

Based on this information, I can identify the dog breed that could be right for me.

Dog Breed	Easy to Train	Activity Level	Care and Grooming	Deal Breakers?
1				
2				
3				

The dog breed that is best for me is probably:

Because:

106 • Come to Life! Your Guide to Self-Discovery

Activity 5D

Buffet of Options

How do you know if you will like a food that you have not tasted before? How can you explore new food options rather than always eating the same things? What are some healthy food options you could add to your diet? Here's an activity and *Buffet of Options* infographic to help you learn more about flavors, textures and ingredients that you might like.

1. Go to a buffet restaurant. Before you have your regular meal, make yourself a "sampler plate." Put a small spoonful or mini-serving of five new foods on your plate. (Be sure to avoid any foods with ingredients you are allergic to!)
2. Fill out the infographic with the names of the five foods.
3. Before you taste each food, predict whether or not you are going to like it.
4. Taste each food and decide if you actually like it or not.
5. If you don't like a food, can you explain why? (Texture, smell, spice, etc.)
6. Of the new foods you tasted, which one do you like best?
7. What else did you learn from doing this activity?
8. How is this process like making other choices about your life?

Activity 5D

e³ = Explore. Experience. Evolve.
Buffet of Options

How do I know if I will like a food that I haven't tasted before? This activity can help me learn about flavors, textures and ingredients I like or don't like.

1. I will go to a local buffet restaurant. Before I have my regular meal, I'll make myself a "sampler plate." I'll put a small spoonful or mini-serving of five new foods on my plate. (I'll be sure to avoid any foods with ingredients I'm allergic to!)
2. I will list the five foods on this infographic.
3. Before I taste each food, I'll predict whether or not I am going to like it.
4. I'll taste each food and decide if I actually like it or not.
5. I'll explain why I like or don't like something (texture, smell, spice, etc.).
6. I'll sum up with a food I would be willing to eat again in the future (if there is one), and something I learned about myself by doing this activity.

Food to Taste	Will I Like It?	Do I Like It?	Why or Why Not?
1			
2			
3			
4			
5			

Of the five new foods I tasted, I would be willing to eat this food again in the future:

I learned something new about myself from doing this activity:

Activity 5E

Anywhere On Earth

Is there a place you would love to go on a vacation? Some place you have dreamed of visiting? If the answer is, "Yes," great! If you have never traveled away from home or have never been on a vacation, you might say, "I don't know."

In this activity you'll go online to research what is involved in taking a one-week vacation to three different destinations of your choice. You can learn a lot from this decision-making exercise and see how the process can help you with real decisions you need to make. We've provided an infographic, *Anywhere on Earth*, that you can use for this activity.

Remember, you are not really taking a trip or buying a vacation, so DO NOT pay any money or use a credit card for this exercise!

1. Pick three places you might like to visit (maybe the place where one of your favorite movies or TV shows was filmed, the setting of a favorite book, a theme park, or another place you've heard about). Write these place names in the first column on the infographic.

2. Pretend your budget is $5,000, to cover your travel, hotel, meals and activities. Pick a particular week of the year for your visit (because prices are different at different times). Learn what your $5,000 could buy at the three destinations. Compare the three options using the infographic or write your own notes.

3. Visit a travel site like TripAdvisor.com to see what other travelers have to say about the three destinations. Based on their ratings *and* the costs you have learned about, give the options you have written on your infographic one to five stars.

4. Use the infographic to pick your pretend destination based on what seems to be the best fit for you.

5. What else did you learn from doing this activity?

6. How is this process like making other choices about your life?

Chapter Five • 109

Anywhere on Earth

It can be fun to pick a destination to visit some day and learn from the experience.

1. I'll go online to research taking a one-week vacation, pretending my budget is $5,000 to cover my travel, hotel, meals and activities. I'll pick a particular week of the year to research three different destinations of my choice (because prices are different at different times). I'll learn what my money could buy at the three locations (but I will NOT really buy a vacation!). I'll take notes and use this infographic to compare the three options.

2. Next, I'll visit a travel site like TripAdvisor.com to see what other travelers have to say about the three destinations. Based on their ratings, I'll give the options on this infographic one to five stars.

3. I'll use the infographic to pick my pretend destination based on what seems to be the best fit for me. I'll tell why it is a good choice for me.

Place to go	Airfare or travel cost	Hotel and meals	Activities to do	Star ratings
1				
2				
3				

Of these three choices, the best place to pretend to go on vacation would be:

This option is best because:

Activity 5F

Pick a Color

You read about the *Color of Choice* activity earlier in this chapter. It is eye-opening to actually go through the process. Here are the steps for another version of the activity that stops before you put any paint on the walls. Of course, really picking a color and painting a room is a great idea if that was something you (and your family) want to do anyway.

	Pick a Color
	1. Pick a particular room in your house that you want to repaint for the purpose of this activity (but not in real life).
	2. Ask a friend, family member, teacher or other ally to go to the paint or home improvement store with you.
	3. When you get to the wall of paint chips, stand back and look at all them all to see what colors (if any) jump out at you. Narrow down your preference to a color family (a rainbow color: red, orange, yellow, green, blue, indigo or violet).
	4. Pick three or four of your favorite options within the color family and take those paint chips.

Chapter Five • 111

Activity 5F (continued)

5. Ask your companion to also pick three or four color options within the color family that he or she thinks would be good choices and take those paint chips, too.

6. Go home and look at your paint chips in the room to be painted. Check out how each option works and with other things in your environment (especially things you don't want to change like carpet and furniture). Select a favorite.

7. Check out your companion's choices. Are any of his or her picks a good match? Do you like any of your companion's choices better than yours?

8. Between your choices and your companion's choices, pick a color. Make the choice you think is best for you.

9. What did you learn from doing this activity? How is this process like making other choices about your life?

Resources

Websites — There are a lot of interesting resources online that can help you explore the ideas from this chapter. Here are a few suggestions.

- The Society for Human Resource Management offers a directory of job titles with duties involved in the jobs. This can help you figure out if your current skill set matches jobs you might be interested in, and can give you an idea of skills you may need to build.
https://www.shrm.org/templatestools/samples/jobdescriptions/pages/bytitle.aspx

- Dr. Hossein Arsham of the University of Baltimore shares a list of resources about "decision science" based on extensive research behind how people make choices and solve problems.
http://home.ubalt.edu/ntsbarsh/business-stat/refop.htm

- There's an app you can use to analyze the benefits (pros) and the drawbacks (cons) of a decision you are currently thinking about. Based on the details you provide, the app will mathematically calculate total points so that you can arrive at an informed decision. http://www2.elc.polyu.edu.hk/cill/tools/prosandcons.htm

- Best-selling author, teacher and life coach Shannon Kaiser reveals three things you can do to instantly get an idea of what your purpose in life is, and what you can do to start serving that purpose. http://www.huffingtonpost.com/shannon-kaiser/3-unexpected-ways-to-find_b_5176511.html

- If you are not sure what college major or career would be good options, this questionnaire will help you determine what jobs or fields of study might be best for you to pursue based on your interest in various topics. It only takes about three minutes to take it, and it's free.
http://www.yourfreecareertest.com/

- The *Occupational Outlook Handbook* from the U.S. Bureau of Labor Statistics is a great free tool to help with career exploration and decision-making. http://www.bls.gov/ooh. You and your allies can learn about job duties, pay and work environment for careers you might be interested in.

- For more information on specific careers or jobs, O*NET OnLine gives detailed descriptions of many different jobs or positions. It explains the kind of technology, tasks and activities are involved in doing them. The site also lists the skills and abilities that are usually required for specific jobs.
  http://www.onetonline.org/

- The U.S. Bureau of Labor Statistics website pages "For Students" can help students learn about different careers, explore the kind of jobs that match talents and interests, watch videos and find other resources.
  http://www.bls.gov/k12/

Videos — Here are a few suggestions of online videos that can help you explore the ideas from this chapter.

- The Travelindex Network and The Travel & Tourism Foundation put together a video describing how taking a journey to another place is more than just being on a trip…it is taking an opportunity to look inside yourself.
  https://www.youtube.com/watch?v=TKzW3WjIWnY

- If you are looking for a new start in life or are not sure where to start, access career aptitude tests via www.mysecretpotential.com and get answers to your questions about what you want to do with your life!
  https://www.youtube.com/watch?v=uuH-WMDNdCM

- Andrea Cairella, CLPP, of True Potential Counseling, offers valuable decision-making skills for your personal and professional life.
  https://www.youtube.com/watch?v=CLKvmAaGD8k

- Comedian and talk show host Ellen DeGeneres offers humor behind realistic but complicated decisions that we make every single day.
  https://www.youtube.com/watch?v=BatqV3B9hiU

- Success coach Tony Robbins discusses the importance of decision-making and the power associated with it.
  https://www.youtube.com/watch?v=Q6y4ryYQPJo

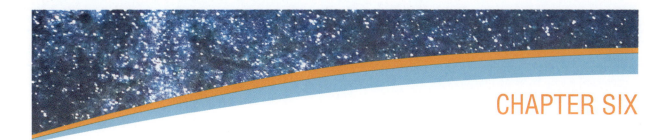

CHAPTER SIX

Find Your Voice

This chapter is about your power to control your own life. Each of us has the power to become our best self. You have the power to find your own happiness. You just have to be brave enough to take steps in that direction, even if it is not easy. Knowing that your hard work can help you get something you want can help you stick with it.

We'll talk about things you can do to take responsibility for your future. You can learn to trust in your abilities and tell yourself, "I know I can do it!" Especially if you have ASD, ADHD or another disability, we'll explain how you can evolve into a self-advocate who is prepared to speak up for yourself in planning for the future. We hope that this entire book is a helpful tool in your own journey to become a self-advocate. It's encouraging to know that young people who get help to learn **self-advocacy** skills are more successful as adults than those who don't.

Check out the infographic *I Can and I Will!*. It will remind you of the meaning of *self-efficacy*, *self-determination* and *self-advocacy*, and why they matter to you.

Becoming a Self-Advocate

In my very last team meeting as I was being exited from special education services, the transition specialist said, "Remember, Tom, to be successful in life, you have to understand autism, know how it affects you, know what kind of help you need, and know how to ask for it." She was telling me how to be a self-advocate. While this was some of the best advice I ever got, the reality is that I was not prepared to do those things.

	I Can and I Will!	
TERM	**WHAT IT MEANS**	**BENEFIT TO ME**
Self-Efficacy	Belief in my power to control different aspects of my own life. I can have an effect on how things turn out.	Believing in my own ability to do what I need to do helps me reach my goals.
Self-Determination	Being in charge of my own life, especially when considering goals, options and choices.	Empowers me to make decisions, work towards my goals, be more independent and feel more confident.
Self-Advocacy	Learning to speak up for myself in a respectful way to direct my own life. Finding information, knowing my responsibilities and rights. Knowing who can help me when I need help.	I can discover my own voice and my own power to get what I need. I may feel happier and more in control of my life.

I wish I had learned about self-advocacy years earlier than I did, to have more time to develop the skills I needed. It took a lot of effort to develop in these areas, but now these abilities are part of my life and I use them regularly.

It is a good idea to talk with your allies to identify your needs in the area of self-advocacy. Check out the infographic *Finding My Voice* to learn about some of the skills that self-advocates use. Identify some goals for yourself in this area. Then make a plan so that you can learn and practice these skills, too!

Finding My Voice
Self-advocacy Means I Can:

	**Speak up for myself** • Share my likes, dislikes, needs, hopes and dreams • Explain what others need to know about me • Ask for help when I need it • Agree or disagree with others in a respectful way
	**Get the information I need** • Research and explore • Find answers that I am looking for • Ask questions • Ask for help from people with experience
	**Listen and learn** • Listen to input and feedback from others • Consider the advice of people who care about me • Learn from people who have years of life experience
	**Make decisions about my life** • Explore options • Think through possible choices and how they could affect me (and others) • Make sure my likes and dislikes are part of conversations and plans for the future
	**Problem-solve** • Think of possible solutions • Think through possible outcomes for different options before picking a solution • Ask others for help when needed

Many of these things should make sense because we have explored them in other chapters of the book. Some of these ideas may still be confusing, but remember, self-advocates do not have to do everything alone. Your allies (parents, teachers, siblings, agency staff, etc.) can be part of your journey.

Chapter Six • 117

Self-advocacy also includes partnering with others to:

- Know your rights and responsibilities
- Figure out who will support you in your journey
- Reach out when you need help or support

We'll talk more about these things in this chapter. You can also learn more from some of the resources listed at the end of the chapter.

Self-Awareness and Self-Advocacy

If you are self-aware, you can be a stronger self-advocate. That is one of the reasons we dedicate so many chapters in this book to the process of self-discovery.

- You have to know yourself well to understand what you want and need.
- Understanding your strengths can help you identify the skills and abilities you can use to build your success.
- Knowing what works for you is important in deciding if the ideas or solutions that may be suggested are likely to be a good fit for you (or not).

For example, a young man named Kevin was having trouble arriving on time to work. He wanted a way to be more organized and asked a teacher for help. His teacher suggested writing things down on a calendar because that is what worked for her. Kevin did that, but it did not help him be on time.

One day, Kevin was telling a coworker about the situation and she showed him how to use his Smartphone to set alarms and reminders like she did. Kevin loved using his Smartphone, which made this solution a good fit. This option had good results, and he was on time to work.

That's what we mean when we say that self-awareness helps you know if an idea or solution is right for you, or not. When people want to be helpful, they might suggest ideas that work for them. When you know yourself, you can pick the options that are likely to be the best fit for you.

Be Involved in Your Individualized Education Plan (IEP)

Self-advocates need to understand that you have the power to control your life and make choices that move you in the direction you want to go, to help you be your best self. If you receive special education services in school, you probably have an Individualized Education Plan, or IEP. Even if you don't have an IEP or are not in school anymore, there may be some interesting things to know in this section, so please read on.

Usually, parents and teachers take the lead in developing the IEP. It includes:

- Information about your areas of need
- Goals to work on
- Services or supports to help you reach your goals
- Accommodations that you need (like more time to finish an assignment or a quiet place to take tests)

- Modifications to your education (like reduced number of assignments).

As you work towards a more independent and productive life, you need to understand how to read your IEP. And not only that! You have the right to be involved in your IEP and the decisions made about you. You can have a say in what courses you want to take, what job you want to do in the future or where you want to live, just to name a few things. If you do not speak up for yourself, you risk *not* living the life that YOU want.

That is why it is important for YOU to be involved in your IEP meeting, whether it is for a short time or the entire meeting. That way, you will know what is being discussed. You can agree or disagree with any parts of the plan. Be sure to take the chance to explain to your IEP team what is or is not working for you. The team can stop doing things that are not working for you and reshape the plan to result in greater success.

Chapter Six • 119

Take Your Time

When I was a freshman in high school, I started slowly by attending my IEP meetings for just a few minutes. Over time, I stayed for more of the meeting and learned to become a more active part of the team. My mom and I planned and practiced ahead of time what I would do and say. This way I felt prepared and knew what to expect. When there was something I did not understand or did not agree with, I felt confident about speaking up. Eventually, I was able to take a leadership role in my meetings.

I remember one situation when some test results showed I had a great vocabulary and good reading comprehension. However, another test showed I was doing very poorly in the same areas. I had to ask the team, "Which is it?" to clear up the confusion. By asking questions about the tests and what the results meant, I was able to understand more. It made my IEP more meaningful to me.

Being actively involved in your IEP is a great way to develop self-advocacy skills. Again, you do not have to take on everything at once. Let your teachers and parents teach you about the plan and guide you in the process.

You can start by participating at a level you are comfortable with and get more involved over time. If something works for you and is going well, feel free to say so. If a particular service or situation is not working for you, say something about it. At the end of the day, it is YOUR life that will change because of what happens with the IEP. Being involved can result in change for the better.

As important as a regular IEP is, it is important to work with your IEP team to figure out a *transition plan*. This plan helps you to successfully adjust from high school to college, from your parents' house to your own place, from school to work, etc. Your team needs to know what you want so they can prepare you for the future.

Another name for high school is secondary school. Post-secondary goals are goals you want for yourself once you leave high school. We have already begun exploring these things in other parts of the book, which might help you have a better idea of what you want for yourself.

Please check out the infographic called *Post-Secondary Goals*. This is a great page to complete with a trusted adult and share with your IEP team. This way you can let the team know the answers to the important questions that are at the heart of transition plans.

Post-Secondary Goals What do I want to do after I leave high school?			
	Question	Yes or No?	More information about my plans
	Do I plan to live on my own at some time after high school?		If I'm going to live on my own (even in a college dorm), I can tell my IEP team so I can get help to build the skills I need.
	Will I continue my education (sometimes called post-secondary education)?		If I tell my IEP team that I plan to continue my education after high school, they can help me with enrollment and can work on skills needed for success.
	Do I want to get a job at some time after high school?		If I say "yes" to work, I can do career exploration and have real work experience in high school.

When the IEP team knows what you want and need, they can

- Help you build skills
- Provide work experiences outside of school
- Fill out paperwork
- Take other steps needed to help you achieve your goals.

The team can also connect you and your family with resources or other agencies that can support your plans. People from those agencies can join your transition team while you are still in high school. This can help make the transition to life after high school smoother and more successful.

When You Turn 18

You have the right to advocate for getting your needs met, but there's a lot of work involved in learning self-advocacy and self-determination skills. It takes time, practice and support. When you are younger than age 18, your parents (or guardian) have the legal right to make decisions for you.

Once you turn 18, you are legally considered an adult. Many legal rights transfer to you at 18, including the right (and responsibility) of making decisions. Check out the infographic *Student Bill of Rights*. It sums up some of the most important educational rights you have in your IEP meetings once you turn 18.

Student Bill of Rights
My Rights When I Turn 18 (also called "reaching the age of majority")
I have the right to:
Know what my disability is and how it affects my ability to learn, live independently, and work
Be provided with information regarding assessment, services and my Individualized Education Program (IEP) in a language and format that I understand
Participate in my IEP meetings
Have individuals who understand me and my disability serve on my IEP team
Accept or **refuse** services
Disagree with any part of my IEP, and receive help in writing a complaint, requesting mediation, or asking for a due process hearing
Adapted with permission from *Transition to Adult Living: An Information and Resource Guide* (CalSTAT, 2007)

Rights are not the only thing that transfer to you when you turn 18. Check out the infographic *Student Bill of Responsibilities* to learn about the responsibilities that also transfer to you!

Student Bill of Responsibilities My Responsibilities When I Turn 18 (also called "reaching the age of majority")	
It is my responsibility to:	
	Ask questions until I understand
	Attend all meetings and actively participate in planning for my adult life
	Invite people I trust and who know me well to IEP meetings (such as parents, friends, grandparents, coaches or teachers)
	Understand that refusing services may affect my school program (and work program if I have one) and that I may not get these services back
	Follow through and be cooperative with any process or service that I request
Adapted with permission from *Transition to Adult Living: An Information and Resource Guide* (CalSTAT, 2007)	

Sharing Your Rights

Did it seem confusing when you read about rights and responsibilities? These ideas can seem complicated. It can be a good idea to keep your parents or caregivers involved in your educational planning and decision-making, especially if you don't feel ready to be in charge of planning and decision-making when you turn 18 (or since you turned 18 if you already had your 18th birthday).

Chapter Six • 123

We'll explain more about how and why to share your rights in the following section, *When You Turn 18, Share Your Rights*. You can also discuss this with parents, caregivers or teachers, and learn more from the resources at the end of this chapter.

When You Turn 18, Share Your Rights

Did you know that you become a legally responsible adult at the age of 18? Many rights and responsibilities transfer to you. Even though you have the right to be in charge of your IEP, you do not have to handle it alone. In fact, it might be wise to share your IEP rights with your parents or caregivers.

How do you share your educational rights with your parents or guardians? You just have to sign and date a piece of paper called a "release" that says you want to share your rights with your parents or another trusted adult. Once you leave school, you can also sign a release that allows your parents to be involved in certain aspects of your work or college experiences, like helping you sign up at the Center for Disabilities at college.

Some people may be surprised to learn that you want to share your rights with your parents. Many believe that just because the calendar says we are adults, we have to be fully responsible for ourselves. Expecting us to meet the demands of adulthood when we turn 18 may not be realistic if we are still developing skills to handle adult life. In fact, it can be a big source of anxiety to be asked to do more than we are actually ready to do.

This can be especially true for students on the autism spectrum who often have social-communication challenges. For example, a young man with ASD that I know had a lot of anxiety about talking to strangers. The Department of Disabled Student Services at college required that he give his self-disclosure letter and request for accommodations to each professor on his own. He felt too anxious, so he didn't do it. As a result, he went through the semester without communicating his needs to his teachers and ended up failing his courses.

You may want to learn more about sharing your rights and the proper ways to do it, for education and other areas of life. Talk to your parents or teachers to learn more about the process. Some of the resources at the end of the chapter may also be helpful.

Understand Accommodations and Modifications

Knowing yourself includes understanding different aspects of your disability, how they affect you, and the kind of help you might need (depending on the situation). Almost every student with an IEP has *accommodations* and *modifications* in their plan, but many of us don't know what this means.

The infographic *Understanding Accommodations and Modifications* explains what these words mean. The information is adapted from FAPE, Families and Advocates Partnership for Education, found at http://www.wrightslaw.com/info/fape.accoms.mods.pdf.

\	Understanding Accommodations and Modifications	
TERM	**WHAT IT MEANS**	**BENEFIT TO ME**
Accommodation	A change that enables me to complete the same task as others, by changing *how* I do it. This means changing the amount of time, the place where I do it, how information is presented to me, and/or the way I respond. Examples include getting extra time to take tests or wearing headphones to reduce noise.	I can complete the task I need to do without changing the task itself.
Modification	An adjustment to an assignment or test that changes *what* I am supposed to do or learn. An example is getting an *alternate assignment* that is easier to complete than the "standard" work that others are doing.	I can complete the task by changing it in some way.

Chapter Six • **125**

Here are a few more concrete examples of accommodations and modifications that may be part of your special education or 504 plan at school.

Accommodations		Modifications
Do the same homework as classmates, but type it on a computer		Do different homework than other students in my grade do (easier or shorter)
Have more time to complete a project		Do a different project than other students
Take the same test as everyone else, but use a calculator or electronic dictionary		Have fewer questions on a test, or take a different test than other students

Both accommodations and modifications may be used while you are in high school. It is a good idea to know which ones are being used for you, why you need them and how they help you.

Why? Because once you turn 18 and/or leave school, it will be up to YOU to ask for the accommodations you need in higher education (like college or job training). You will have to ask your employer for accommodations or modifications in the workplace. It is easier to get accommodations or modifications if you can explain *what* they are and *why* you need them.

When you leave school, the district draws up a document called a Summary of Performance (SOP) to use in life after high school. Every student in special education is supposed to have an SOP. It sums up many things about you, including the accommodations and modifications you need. You can give input to help write the SOP.

I worked with my IEP team to learn about the kinds of accommodations that helped me. My accommodations were included in the SOP. I practiced explaining why I needed the things listed (like a quiet testing environment).

My SOP was extremely helpful to me to move from high school, to community college, to a university. You will want to talk more about accommodations, modifications and your SOP with your allies.

More About Self-Disclosure

Without going too much into the law, once you are an adult (age 18), you need to have some way to explain your disability to employers, professors or even police officers to help them understand your needs. This is how you can get the modifications and accommodations you need in your work, learning or life environment. The infographic *What is Self-Disclosure?* explains more about this.

What is Self-Disclosure?		
TERM	**WHAT IT MEANS**	**BENEFIT TO ME**
Self-Disclosure I HAVE...	Explaining my disability to employers, professors, agency staff or even police officers to help them understand my needs. There are different ways to self-disclose like safely presenting a disclosure card, wearing a medical alert tag, filling out a form, or just talking.	I may get modifications, accommodations and other protections of the Americans with Disabilities Act (ADA) or laws called Section 504 to help me in college, work or the community.

Many of the activities in this book have helped you identify your needs. It is a good idea to practice explaining what you need in different everyday situations. You can start small, like letting your family know you need some quiet time so you can study. Being aware of your needs and sharing this information are skills that can help you for the rest of your life.

I have a lot of practice disclosing that I have autism to professors and employers. I also have a way to tell the police that I have autism so they can help me better. I carry a folding card in my wallet that says, "I have autism." When a police officer asks for my driver's license, I ask if I can also give him or her a card about my disability.

The outside of the card explains what autism is. The inside of the card is customized to let the officer know specific ways to help me (slowing things down, using clear language, etc.). The card also includes my parents' contact information. You can order a self-disclosure card like this one for autism or other disabilities at www.besafethemovie.com.

Now It's Your Turn

In the process of learning to be a self-advocate and finding your voice, you'll need to learn how to ask for help in appropriate ways, how to solve problems, and how to make decisions. The activities and resources that follow can help you get started.

Activity 6A

Get Information in Advance

Do you read reviews online before you buy a new video game or some other item you are interested in? If you do, you know how much the item costs and where you can buy it. You can read reviews to see what others like and don't like about the item. Gathering facts and opinions helps you make an informed decision.

This everyday example also applies to taking on more responsibility as a self-advocate. Finding the information you need helps you feel more confident and prepared, especially for new situations. When you need information, it is a good idea to research things in advance during a calm time so you can process it all. This is better than figuring things out when you are under pressure.

For example, say you are nervous about going to a community college campus for the first time. You can use technology like Google Earth to take a virtual tour of the place before you actually go there. You can locate particular places, like an office you need to visit or an employment center. Using a virtual map gives you a preview of what the streets and buildings in the area look like. This visual image can help you feel more comfortable when you actually go there.

You may want to learn to use map technology on a computer or Smartphone. A friend or relative who is tech-savvy may be able to help you with this. You can start by using map technology to find the place you live. Then, "visit" a familiar place to see how it looks in the map technology. Finally, pick a place to "virtually visit" anywhere in the world by typing in an address or place name.

Ask the Right Questions

For the longest time, I thought that if I asked questions, it meant that I was stupid. I eventually learned that asking questions is essential for finding the answers I need to make better decisions and live the life I want. The better the question I asked, the more useful the answer. You may find, like I did, that asking questions and understanding "why?" can help you to:

- See the reason that things work the way they do,
- Lead to more reasonable decision-making, and
- Open a lot of doors for you in your life.

As a self-advocate, if I need information about a particular topic, I first ask myself, "Who would know the answer to the question(s) I have?" Once I identify somebody and contact them, I explain my situation and ask if they can assist me. If they cannot assist me, I ask them to tell me who they think can. I repeat this procedure until I get the answer(s) I need and resolve the situation.

I came up with the mnemonic (memory aid) **WASP** to help you remember the stages of the process:

What's wrong
Ask for assistance
Seek a solution
Proceed

The next time you have a problem, see if a little WASP can help you resolve it!

Activity 6C

Ask For and Accept Help

Don't be afraid to ask for help! Some people think that asking for help is a sign of weakness. Others feel embarrassed or worry that they will be judged as weak or incompetent. No one has all the answers, and you do not have to be perfect. Even Einstein asked questions!

I put a lot of pressure on myself to be perfect because I thought I was the only one who was not perfect! I thought I had to be perfect because I thought my mom was perfect. When my mom learned about my (false) belief, she let me know that she was not perfect at all. She started talking more about her areas of improvement.

For example, she will tell you she is terrible at reading maps. Before GPS, she got lost a lot and was frustrated. Instead of keeping this situation to herself, she began to explain what was going on when she was lost. She told me what her options were (stop for directions, phone a friend, etc.) and she picked one. Seeing my mom needing help and asking for it helped *me* be more accepting of the fact that no one is perfect and everyone needs help sometimes. I also learned I can rely on other people, and ask them for help to reach my goals.

Don't be ashamed to ask your allies for the help you need whether it is emotional support, practical advice, relationship building, skill development or anything else that can help you be happy and successful. Some day you can return the favor and find out how rewarding it is to help others.

Is there something on your mind that you need help with? You can use the infographic *Who Can Help?* to write down a few things you are thinking, wondering or worrying about. You can list some people who might be able to help you. Then start the conversation. Don't forget to ask, "If you can't help me with this, who can?"

Activity 6C (continued)

Who Can Help?

If I have a worry or problem on my mind, it can be helpful to talk to someone about it.
- Sometimes I just need someone who is a good listener.
- Other times, for problem-solving, it is a good idea to talk with someone who has the power to help, or who can connect me with the right person(s).
- I can write down the name and contact information of someone I can reach out to when I need help, guidance or solutions.

What's on my mind?	Who can I talk to about this?

Activity 6D

Take the Worst-Case Scenario and the Mirror Tests

Before you have to make a choice or take action of some kind, take the time to think it through. In *Chapter Five: Find Yourself*, we explained how making a "Pro and Con" list can help you choose or make an informed decision. This strategy helps me feel more confident when making a decision and it may be a good tool for you, too.

Another strategy I use when making some decisions is to consider the "worst-case scenario." I ask myself, "What is the worst thing that could happen if I do (or don't do) this?" For example, if I am debating whether I should ask a girl out, I ask myself, "What is the worst thing that can happen if I ask her out?" Answer: She could say "no." Knowing that I could handle being turned down encourages me to take the risk and hope it works out. In fact, 99% of the time, the answer is that if the proposed action is not successful, it will not kill me nor will it be "the end of the world."

The Mirror Test is another useful strategy. Before making a decision, I ask myself if I would be able to look at myself in the mirror and live with my decision. Looking in the mirror means that you consider the way the decision impacts you and others, and whether the decision is hurtful or harmful. If I would feel guilty or bad about a decision I make or could not live with myself (and look at myself in the mirror), I would not take that course of action.

Do you have a decision you need to make in the near future? Even for a small choice, you can use all three of these strategies to see if they are helpful. Practicing will help you figure out which one(s) you like best.

Activity 6E

Generate Options

There is more than one way to solve just about any problem. To solve a problem or get out of a difficult situation, it helps to know what options are available to you. Let's take the example of what to do if you are lost in an unfamiliar place. Options include:

- Ask someone for directions
- Pull out a paper map
- Use your phone to locate your position and where you want to go
- Call someone for help

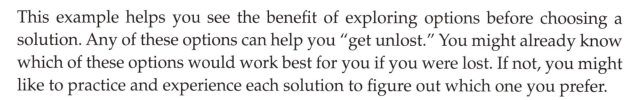

This example helps you see the benefit of exploring options before choosing a solution. Any of these options can help you "get unlost." You might already know which of these options would work best for you if you were lost. If not, you might like to practice and experience each solution to figure out which one you prefer.

To learn to generate options, start by remembering a situation in the past when you successfully generated options to solve a problem (on your own or with help). If you can't remember, ask your parents or a teacher to remind you of a situation when this happened. Write down what the situation was, the options you had, and the solution you chose.

Knowing that you have successfully generated options in the past can help you feel more confident in your ability to generate options and solve problems in other challenging situations. You can also talk with an ally to plan and practice generating options for future problems or choices. Examples include generating options for what to do if you are delayed getting to work or school, what to do if your car breaks down or what to do if you lose your cell phone. When the time comes, you will have your options ready and be able to choose one that works for you!

Activity 6F

Always Have a Plan B

When I was in a social skills group, I heard about some young men that planned to go see the latest action hero movie. However, when they got to the movie theater, the show was sold out. They didn't know what else to do, so they decided to just go home. What a waste! They could have seen another movie, hung out somewhere else or made their own fun!

When things do not go the way you planned, you are faced with an unexpected (and potentially stressful) situation. It is a good idea to make a "Plan B"; that is, deciding in advance what you will do if your original plan does not work out. Knowing you have another good option ready (or even a third choice, "Plan C") can be very calming.

In another example, say you take the bus on a regular basis and are used to a particular schedule and route. What if there is a shutdown of a major road and the bus cannot get through? How would you get home?

It is a good idea to think about things that might disrupt your regular plan and come up with "Plan B" in advance, when things are calm and you have time to think, talk things over with others and figure it out. Then, when something unexpected happens, you can stay calmer and feel more secure knowing that you have "Plan B" ready to go.

Next time you make a plan to do something, also come up with your "Plan B" (and even "Plan C") in advance. Then you'll be ready with an option that works for you if "Plan A" doesn't work out.

Activity 6G

Apply the Test of Evidence (TOE)

Many people with ASD have a tendency to focus on facts and rules. This is sometimes called black-and-white thinking. Unfortunately, black-and-white thinking can cause someone to get stuck on certain ideas. Once they are stuck, it is hard to change their mind.

The Test of Evidence is a strategy you can use to think about information if you are feeling stuck on an idea, or if someone else tells you that you seem stuck. TOE is an objective way to look at information that supports your beliefs *and* any facts that contradict it (Friedberg & McClure, 2015).

- First, you write down "confirming evidence," things that support your belief.

- Then, you list any "disconfirming evidence," things that do *not* support your belief.

- Finally, you can look at all the information together, and draw a new conclusion if the facts point in that direction.

Using the TOE to look at the facts can help you consider new ideas and even change your mind about something.

TOE is one example of the kind of tools used in cognitive behavioral intervention (CBI), also called cognitive behavioral therapy. It is a form of mental health therapy that helps clients solve problems and take action.

CBI can be helpful for different aspects of self-development such as replacing negative thinking with positive attitudes, managing stress and improving self-regulation. CBI has the potential to help individuals on the spectrum or with other special needs handle challenges and improve quality of life. You and your allies may want to learn more about it and find CBI providers in your area.

Check out the following example that demonstrates how to use the Test of Evidence.

Activity 6G (continued)

Test of Evidence (TOE) Example

My Belief: I will never move out of my family home and live on my own.

Evidence That Supports My Belief	Evidence That Does Not Support My Belief
I have been living with my parents for 24 years so that is likely to continue forever.	Many young people live with their parents into their 20s but make a change in their late 20s or their 30s.
I don't know how to do any household chores.	I learned about expiration dates on food and can cook a few different meals.
I don't have anywhere else to go.	I have a friend who lives in his own apartment; maybe I can find a place, too.

New Conclusion:

Someday I will move out of my family home and live on my own. In the meantime, I can keep that goal in mind, work on more skills to live independently and learn about places I might be able to live when I move out.

You can use the *Test of Evidence* infographic to test all kinds of ideas you may have. You can practice with a simple belief before you use it with a more serious or difficult belief that you might be struggling with.

Chapter Six • 137

Activity 6G (continued)

Test of Evidence (TOE) Example

My Belief:

Evidence That Supports My Belief	Evidence That Does Not Support My Belief

Activity 6H

The Answer Is "No"

When I was growing up, I spent a lot of energy attempting to please others. As a result, I sometimes made choices that made other people happy but did not make me happy. Situations ranged from simple things like what clothes to wear, to more complicated things like who to date. Sometimes I said "yes" to things because I thought people would like me. For example, if someone asked to borrow my stuff, I would say "yes," even though I really wanted to say "no."

As I became a self-advocate, I realized that I did not always have to make everyone else happy. Finding the strength to say "no" when I needed to was liberating and empowering.

On the flip side of saying "no," sometimes you have to be ready to take "no" for an answer. Even though you have the right to speak up for yourself, you may not always get the results you want. It is important to know this in advance and prepare yourself to deal with it.

For example, many young adults and their families are shocked to find out that there is no federal law requiring that services be provided to every adult with disabilities who needs or asks for them. That is, once a young person exits high school, different laws apply. Service agencies can turn you down. College professors can tell you that they will not honor your requests for accommodations because they are not reasonable. These types of situations can be a rude awakening. This brings me to the next point …

Activity 6I

Learn About the Law

It is important to learn about key rights you may have in different situations, like the right to disagree with an educational plan or the right to appeal when you are turned down for certain services. You need to know about laws that apply when you are in special education (IDEA). There are laws that protect individuals with disabilities from discrimination in the workplace or higher education (the Americans with Disabilities Act (ADA, 2008), and Section 504 of the Rehabilitation Act (1973).

Many websites offer this information and we list several options in the resources section of this chapter. Youthood.org offers information that is written with youth in mind, at https://www.youthhood.org/government/rd_ada.asp. You will probably need help from someone who can explain these laws to you and guide you to take the steps needed to protect yourself from discrimination related to your disability.

Resources

Websites — There are a lot of interesting resources online that can help you and your allies further explore the ideas from this chapter. Here are a few suggestions.

- The meaning of self-determination is explored with illustrations and visual aids.
  http://study.com/academy/lesson/self-determination-theory-capacity-strategy-control-beliefs.html

- *Youthhood* is a free online resource from the University of Minnesota that offers information and activities to help young people figure out the direction they want to take in life and make informed choices. User registration is needed to access the site.
  http://www.youthhood.org/index.asp

- *Opening Doors to Self-Determination Skills: Planning for Life After High School* by the Wisconsin Department of Public Instruction (2013). This 26-page handbook speaks directly to youth and guides you in developing self-determination and self-advocacy skills. Areas covered include possible goals, problem-solving, tools to create a personal profile and person-centered planning. A free PDF is available at http://files.ctctcdn.com/88c2be7a001/3723af0b-ce16-4a13-aa08-be6f8d79f913.pdf

- The PACER center offers information on self-determination including a 2-page summary of self-advocacy at http://www.pacer.org/parent/php/PHP-c116.pdf

- Lots of links and useful information about self-advocacy are available on the Wrightslaw website.
  http://www.wrightslaw.com/info/self.advocacy.htm#sthash.w1ChUbpN.dpuf

- *The Arc's Self-Determination Scale* by Michael Wehmeyer and Kathy Kelchner (1995). Rate yourself on 72 items to get an overall self-determination score and sub-scores in the areas of autonomy, self-regulation, psychological empowerment and self-realization. Free.
  http://www.thearc.org/document.doc?id=3670

- An 11-page guide called *A Student's Guide to the IEP* by Marcy McGahee-Kovac is free to download at the National Information Center for Children and Youth with Disabilities website.
  http://www.php.com/sites/default/files/student_guide_IEP.pdf

- An informative guide to help understand disability rights under Section 504 of the Rehabilitation Act of 1973 can be found at http://www.hhs.gov/sites/default/files/knowyourrights504adafactsheet.pdf
  - Further explanation is available at
    https://www.disability.gov/rehabilitation-act-1973/
  - Text of the law is available at
    http://www2.ed.gov/policy/speced/reg/narrative.html

- A free guide called *The 411 on Disability Disclosure: A Workbook for Youth with Disabilities* is available from the National Collaborative on Workforce and Disability for Youth. Unit 4: Appendix A, "Basic Facts about the Americans with Disabilities Act" may be particularly informative. Download the 99-page guide or individual chapters at
  http://www.ncwd-youth.info/411-on-disability-disclosure

- Consultants from the Job Accommodation Network (JAN) provide guidance regarding ADA's definition of reasonable accommodation to individuals with disabilities, their family members, employers and professionals. It offers an extensive list of the kinds of accommodations that someone with might need in the workplace, including specific accommodations for autism, at http://askjan.org/media/ASD.html

- "Help Your Young Adult Learn About Accessing Accommodations After High School" is available from the Pacer Center at http://www.pacer.org/transition/resource-library/publications/NPC-18.pdf

Videos — Here are a few suggestions of online videos that can help you explore the ideas from this chapter.

- Captain Kirk and Mr. Spock cartoon characters explain self-determination and self-advocacy.
  https://www.youtube.com/watch?v=lLKDE0_fjJk

- Lori LeBrun, Rhode Island's School Counselor of the Year in 2012, created a PowerPoint presentation of helpful hints for self-advocacy at school for students in junior high school and up.
  https://www.youtube.com/watch?v=YCziz9XGUNo

- A 2012 video by the Autism Research Institute of a panel of adult self-advocates, featuring Dr. Stephen Shore.
  https://www.autism.com/services_self-advocacy

- A description of the Autism Self-Advocacy Network and links to various resources on how to improve self-advocacy in young adults with autism.
  https://www.youtube.com/user/autselfadvocacyntwk

- Siblings of individuals with autism offer their perspective on living and coping with their brother's or sister's quirks.
  http://siblingleadership.org/services-and-supports/self-advocacy-resources/

- Self-determination theory of motivation as it applies to the workplace.
  https://www.youtube.com/watch?v=pskp2rZ94RQ and
  https://www.youtube.com/watch?v=RfX4QFMgb3k

- Self-determination applied to college.
  https://www.youtube.com/watch?v=QLp-7Ylq5sw

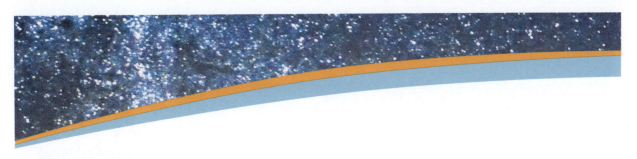

Conclusion

Know Yourself. Love Yourself. Be Yourself. Explore. Experience. Evolve. We hope the information we have shared can help you in the process of self-discovery. All the things you learn about yourself can help you create the life you want. You can find your niche, find your voice and let other people know what you are discovering about yourself.

We have one last activity for you called *I Can Be the Hero in My Own Life*. It's a way to help you organize the information you have discovered about yourself and share it with your allies. This can be a very useful tool for special education meetings or other kinds of future planning. Don't worry if you don't have all the answers yet…complete what you can. Tom filled one out as a model and there is a blank graphic ready for you, too.

I Can Be the Hero in My Own Life

Name	Tom
Date	7/1/17
My best skills: superpowers	Disciplined, determined, high level of integrity, generous
Purpose: what I want to do in life	Help people on a personal level, inspire good, motivate people to be their best self, bring hope to those that need it
Special tools: things that can help me	Social media, writing a book, promotional materials, Web videos
Assets: other things I have going for me	Strong communication skills, leadership abilities, involvement in several non-profit organizations, CPA background

I Can Be the Hero in My Own Life — Tom's Example (continued)

Weakness(es): things that take away my power or distract me from my mission 	Engaging in activities or events that do not line up with my mission to inspire others
Allies: people who can help me 	Mom, Dad, other family members, self-advocates and other friends, Toastmasters Club mentor(s), networking groups, autism societies and organizations, professionals in social media, marketing, etc.
Role model: How is my superhero a good role model for me? 	Seeing what worked for others and doing the kind of things they do will increase my chances of success, outreach and credibility
Other Information: to take into account in planning for my future	I am willing to work hard to achieve what I want in life. I appreciate and thank all the people who helped me in the past and are helping me now.

I Can Be the Hero in My Own Life

Name **Date**	
My best skills: superpowers	
Purpose: what I want to do in life	
Special tools: things that can help me	
Assets: other things I have going for me	

148 • Come to Life! Your Guide to Self-Discovery

Weakness(es): things that take away my power or distract me from my mission	
Allies: people who can help me	
Role model: How is my superhero a good role model for me?	
Other Information: to take into account in planning for my future	

What's Next?

When you are mapping out a path to your future, you will want to figure out how to get from where you are to where you want to go in life. You will want to be in the driver's seat, but you will also want caring adults to help you along the way. You can think of them as the navigators, mechanics and pit crew for your journey. They are your allies and your team.

We hope that the process of self-discovery helps you and your allies prepare you for the future, especially in the special education transition process. Your allies will probably need to take the lead on managing the transition process, but YOU will be at the center of the plan, taking your life in the direction that is right for YOU so that **YOU can come to life!**

References

California Services for Technical Assistance and Training (CalSTAT). (2007). *Transition to adult living: An information and resource guide.* Rohnert Park, CA: California Institute on Human Services.

Friedberg, R.D. & McClure, J.M. (2015). *Clinical practice of cognitive therapy with children and adolescents: The nuts and bolts, second edition.* Guilford: New York.

Iland, E. (2014a). *Be safe teaching edition: Lessons, activities, games and materials to teach teens and adults how to interact safely with the police.* Santa Clarita, CA: Camino Cinema.

Iland, E. (2011) *Drawing a blank: Improving comprehension for readers on the autism spectrum.* Shawnee Mission, KS: AAPC.

National Secondary Transition Technical Assistance Center. (2015a). *Aligning evidence-based practices and predictors for post-school success.* Retrieved from http://www.transitionta.org/sites/default/files/postsecondary/AlignEBPP_Resources_PSS_FINAL_2014.pdf

Raymond, J. (2010) *Temple Grandin on her struggles and yak yaks.* Retrieved September 7, 2016 from http://www.nbcnews.com/id/35150832/ns/health-mental_health/t/temple-grandin-her-struggles-yak-yaks/#.V9CqEZgrI2w

Roux, A. M., Shattuck, P. T., Rast, J. E., Rava, J. A., & Anderson, K. A. (2015). *National autism indicators report: Transition into young adulthood.* Philadelphia, PA: Drexel University, Life Course Outcomes Research Program, A. J. Drexel Autism Institute. Retrieved November 24, 2015 from http://drexel.edu/autisminstitute/researchprojects/research/ResearchPrograminLifeCourseOutcomes/IndicatorsReport/#sthash.GhGi8gdU.dpbs

Bibliography

Here are some resources that may be helpful for allies who are assisting youth or adults.

Online

- *Age of Majority: The Transfer of IDEA Rights to Students at Age 18* from the Ask Resource Center (2013) provides a clear explanation of this process, along with other legal issues like adult guardianship and power-of-attorney (2013). http://askresource.org/wp-content/uploads/2014/09/Age-of-Majority-Transfer-of-Rights.pdf

- *A Center for Independent Living* (CIL) is a cross disability, nonprofit agency designed and operated by individuals with disabilities within a local community. CILs provide five core services: information & referral; independent living skills training; individual and systems advocacy; peer counseling and assistance to help youth with significant disabilities transition to postsecondary life. Find a CIL in your area at http://www.ilru.org/projects/cil-net/cil-center-and-association-directory

- *Keeping It Real* from the Boggs Center on Developmental Disabilities at Rutgers University (2005) is a free, 167-page workbook in English or Spanish that helps allies teach high school students with disabilities to understand who they are, what they want to do as adults, what supports will help them achieve their goals and how to advocate effectively. Free workbooks and a parent guide are available as .pdf files at http://rwjms.rutgers.edu/departments_institutes/boggscenter/products/KeepingItRealHowtoGettheSupportsYouNeedfortheLifeYouWant.html

- *ME! Lessons for Teaching Self-Awareness & Self-Advocacy.* Ten free lessons for teaching self-determination skills (including self-advocacy and self-awareness). Available from the University of Oklahoma's Zarrow Center for Learning Enrichment at http://www.ou.edu/content/education/centers-and-partnerships/zarrow/trasition-education-materials/me-lessons-for-teaching-self-awareness-and-self-advocacy.html

- The website for *Person Centered Planning* from the Yang-Tan Institute at Cornell University offers seven free courses, including one on the person-centered planning process. Each brief course includes activities, readings and resources. http://www.personcenteredplanning.org/index.cfm

- *SOCCSS* (Situation, Options, Consequences, Choices, Strategies, Simulations) is a step-by-step problem-solving process developed by Jan Roosa that can help individuals understand social situations and interactions. SOCCSS provides decision-making techniques and helps learners understand that choices have consequences. Find more information and free templates at http://www.ocali.org/project/resource_gallery_of_interventions/page/soccss

- *When You Turn 18: A Survival Guide for Teenagers.* This well-organized tool explains hundreds of laws that apply once someone turns 18 with wording that young people can understand. Download this free educational tool in English or Spanish at http://www.calbar.ca.gov/Public/Pamphlets/WhenYouTurn18.aspx

- The Wrightslaw website from attorneys Pam and Pete Wright provides reliable information about special education law and advocacy to parents, educators, advocates, and attorneys. The *Advocacy Libraries* and *Law Libraries* include thousands of articles, cases and resources on numerous topics.

Books and Publications

- *Ask and Tell: Self-Advocacy and Disclosure for People on the Autism Spectrum.* Authors Ruth Elaine Joyner Hane, Kassiane Sibley, Stephen M. Shore and other self-advocates help people with autism effectively self-advocate and self-disclose in their pursuit of independent, productive, and fulfilling lives. (AAPC, 2004).

- *The Autism Job Club: The Neurodiverse Workforce in the New Normal of Employment.* Authors Michael S. Bernick and Richard Holden offer six strategies to help adults on the spectrum find and keep work in fields suited to their abilities and talents including technology, the Internet and public services (Skyhorse Publishing, 2015).

- *Developing Talents: Careers For Individuals With Asperger Syndrome And High-functioning Autism.* Autism guru Temple Grandin and parent-professional Kate Duffy share their insights about how to reverse unemployment, underemployment and problems keeping a job experienced by many capable individuals on the spectrum. The idea of good fit is explored by looking at jobs that match well to the features of ASD, as well as job models like entrepreneurship (microenterprise). (AAPC, 2008).

- *Empowering Students with Hidden Disabilities: A Path to Pride and Success.* Authors Margo Vreeburg Izzo and LeDerick R. Horne offer guidance to allies andself-advocates that can help prepare young adults for responsible, self-determined adult lives and careers. Topics include promoting disability pride, reducing stigma of hidden disabilities, developing mentoring programs and learning life-skills (Paul H. Brookes, 2016).

- *The Integrated Self-Advocacy ISA Curriculum: A Program for Emerging Self-Advocates With Autism Spectrum and Other Conditions.* This comprehensive curriculum by Valerie Paradiz helps youth and allies explore self-discovery and self-advocacy. The Teacher Edition and Student Workbook offer lesson plans, worksheets and activities to create a personal self-advocacy portfolio. (AAPC Publishing, 2009).

- *The PATH & MAPS Handbook: Person-Centered Ways to Build Community.* Authors John O'Brien, Jack Pierpoint and Lynda Kahn take readers through all the steps to facilitate future planning, using both PATH and MAPS formats (these terms were once acronyms but are now used as words). Both person-centered processes focus on identifying what is most important to the individual and the steps, people, supports and resources that can help them move in a chosen direction (Inclusion Press, 2012).

- *Self-Determination Strategies for Adolescents in Transition.* Authors David Parker, Sharon Field and Alan Hoffman provide information and case studies to illustrate how allies can help students with high-functioning autism and similar disabilities transition to postsecondary education. The book suggests strategies, direct instruction and coaching to support students, while at the same time respecting their right to make decisions and learn from their life experiences (Pro-Ed, 2013).

- The *Starting Line Transition Program* from Ten Sigma introduces students to important transition concepts. The program guides them to identify (and achieve) their own postsecondary goals in the areas of competitive employment, education/training, and independent living. Two consumable student workbooks called *Foundations* and *Fast Track* plus teacher manuals are available in print and in editable PDF through a license program. Learn more at http://tensigma.org/starting-line-transition-program/

About the Authors

THOMAS W. ILAND, B.S., CPA

Tom is a graduate of California State University Northridge and a Certified Public Accountant. He was diagnosed at the age of 13. Since that time, he has worked hard to achieve many of his goals: full-time employment, driving, living in his own apartment and having a girlfriend.

He has extensive, first-hand experience working for companies including Calavo Growers, Tetra Tech, Princess Cruises, Deloitte, The Walt Disney Company, Blockbuster Video, Regal Entertainment Group, and Hollywood Video.

Tom now dedicates himself full-time to public speaking, offering unique insights with heart and humor in his engaging presentations. Tom has presented several keynote presentations on his mantra: Know Yourself. Love Yourself. Be Yourself. Other topics include interacting safely with law enforcement, and telling your child about their disability. He enjoys presenting and training across the country for a variety of organizations including police departments.

An active volunteer, Tom serves on the Board of Directors for non-profit organizations including Santa Clarita Valley Safe Rides, Junior Chamber International Santa Clarita, The Santa Clarita Valley Mayor's Committee for Employment of Individuals With Disabilities and The Art of Autism. He is a division director for District 52 of Toastmasters International, and has recently earned the Distinguished Toastmaster (DTM) award, the highest award in the organization, indicating an outstanding level of achievement in both communication and leadership. Learn more at www.ThomasIland.com.

EMILY ILAND, M.A.

Emily is an award-winning author, advocate, educator, researcher and leader in the autism community. Her son Tom is the inspiration behind her work in special education. Emily is known for her expertise in areas including the transition to adulthood, autism and law enforcement, reading comprehension, and reaching under-served communities.

Emily is an adjunct professor at California State University Northridge in the Department of Special Education. She is an in-demand presenter in English and Spanish across the country and abroad. She particularly enjoys co-presenting with Tom on a wide range of topics ranging from telling your child about their disability to teaching youth to interact safely with the police, and of course, *Come to Life!* Learn more at www.EmilyIland.com.

Other publications by Emily Iland

- *BE SAFE The Movie*. This video modeling DVD shows teens and adults how to interact safely with the police. (Camino Cinema, 2013).

- *BE SAFE Teaching Edition*. Companion curriculum for BE SAFE The Movie, provides differentiated materials to help diverse learners. (Camino Cinema, 2013).

- *CUíDATE: Guía de Enseñanza*. Spanish-language edition of BE SAFE Teaching Edition. (Camino Cinema, 2014).

- *Drawing A Blank: Improving Comprehension for Readers on the Autism Spectrum*. Evidence-based and practical information on reading comprehension and autism (Autism Asperger Publishing Company, 2011).

- *Autism Spectrum Disorders from A to Z*, with Barbara T. Doyle (Future Horizons, 2004). Comprehensive information for parents and professionals.

- *Los Trastornos del Espectro de Autismo de la A a la Z*. Spanish version of *Autism Spectrum Disorders from A to Z* (Emily Iland, Inc., 2005. Now out of print, updated version coming in 2018).